On Hearing of My Mother's Death Six Years After It Happened

A Daughter's Memoir of Mental Illness

LORI L. SCHAFER

ISBN: 1942170467
ISBN-13: 9781942170464

Second Edition

DEDICATION

In memory of Judy Green-Hair.
May she rest in peace.

CONTENTS

CONTENTS

ACKNOWLEDGMENTS

"Moving In, Moving Out, Moving On" originally appeared in *Foliate Oak Literary Magazine* on November 1, 2013.

"Poisoned" received an Honorable Mention in *The Avalon Literary Review*'s Spring 2014 Contest and was published in that issue.

"A Safe Place" originally appeared in *The Write Place in the Write Time* on September 23, 2014.

"Thank You: An Open Letter To Those Who Stood By Me During Mom's Mental Illness" was originally published on *Elizabeth Hein* on November 7, 2014.

"Only a Dream" was originally published on *The Bipolar Maniac* on November 9, 2014.

"On Writing My Memoir" was originally composed for Diane DeBella's #IAmSubject project, making women the subjects of their own lives, and appeared in her anthology on September 13, 2014.

"You Don't Have to Be Mentally Ill to Suffer from the Stigma Associated with Mental Illness" originally appeared on stigmafighters.com on August 31, 2014.

"Hide and Seek" was a finalist for the 2013 *Able Muse* Write Prize for Prose.

"Poisoned" (fictional version) originally appeared in the *Journal of Microliterature* on November 10, 2013.

"Found Money" originally appeared in *Burningword Literary Journal* on September 30, 2013.

"Cranbury, New Jersey" (fictional version) originally appeared in the May 2014 issue of *eFiction* magazine.

The excerpt from "Author Interview with Ognian Georgiev"

ACKNOWLEDGMENTS

originally appeared on *Land of Books* on November 12, 2014.

My mother's obituary was found on www.tributes.com, originally accessed in May 2013.

I am indebted to Ben Sanford for supplying "The Photograph."

With the exception of my name and my mother's, all other names in this memoir have been changed in order to respect the privacy of any third parties who were tangentially involved in our story.

INTRODUCTION AND NOTES ON THE TEXT

I HAVE TAKEN a somewhat radical approach to structure in this memoir. One of the first things you will notice is that it is not in chronological order. There's a simple reason for that. I realized early on that I was incapable of telling my story that way.

Most of the significant events in our lives can be tied to a particular age, a particular year, or perhaps a particular season. These landmarks in time give us frames of reference to which we can look back in later years and reassemble, in our minds, our own personal timelines. But the events upon which most of my story is based transpired within a comparatively short space of time, a time in which I was struggling with an almost insurmountable level of stress and strain. And now, in my attempt to accurately reconstruct my own past, I find myself often unable to identify what happened when. I can say beyond question that "Moving In, Moving Out, Moving On" was the beginning of my story, and of course I also know when it ends. Logically, I know that "Detention" must have occurred sometime before "Escape," and, based on the weather, that "A Safe Place" transpired sometime much later. But when did "Poisoned" take place? I can't even begin to guess. Was the scene at the coffee shop before or after the scene at the motel? When did my mother first steal my bank book? When did I at last steal it back? I can't answer these questions. There is no one to ask.

Recognizing that there were gaping holes in my recollection, my choices were these: to make my best guesses, but ultimately to know that I was falsifying my own account, or to abandon any attempt at a true linear chronology. I have chosen the latter. Rather than mislead the reader by giving the impression that I've told my story from beginning to end, with neat transitions between individual events that

I cannot recall, I've told it the way I actually do remember it: in bits and pieces, in flashbacks between past and present, in stories that end on the page where they end in my mind. My story is segmented and fractured, the way my own recollections are segmented and fractured.

In some ways, it's fitting. I've spent many years trying to make sense of my mother's psychosis, when I know in my mind that there's no sense to make. And perhaps, for the reader, the nature of my experience is more comprehensible by being told in this way. Because this is what it's like, living with a parent with a severe mental illness. You can never settle in and simply get comfortable with the day-to-day; you constantly have to be prepared for sudden changes in your own situation, for starts and stops and deviations that may, without warning, wash away the path you thought you were following. Until one day, you realize – that path never existed.

This expanded version of *On Hearing of My Mother's Death* has been written in answer to the many requests I have received from readers, who have wanted to know more about my childhood and about my mother's pre-illness life. It also contains several additional recollections that have come back to me since the book was first published, as well as new speculations regarding the source and the course of my mother's illness that have occurred to me over the last few years of pondering our story. I have been honored to share that story with such wonderful readers, many of whom have contacted me to express sympathy or solidarity and to share their own similar stories. It has been heartening to me to hear from so many sufferers, and so many survivors, and so many ordinary people who simply wanted to say that they were moved by our story. My most gracious thanks to you all.

DETENTION

"STEINBERG! SCHAFER! DETENTION!" Mr. Cooper shouted furiously, his nearly bald pointed head bristling with a temper I had never witnessed before. That possibly no one had ever witnessed before. Normally he disregarded his students entirely and went on, in spite of the constant conversation and ill-concealed catcalls, with his physics lectures as if the classroom were empty, or perhaps irrelevant in the face of so much captivating science. But today we had somehow pierced the thick shield of his academic armor and prodded him into unanticipated and unheard-of disciplinary action. I testily kicked aside the pile of tiny paper airplanes that had grown at my feet during the course of the class and glared at my friend Josh, the one who'd gotten me in trouble. I was a good student; a nerd, most said. I'd never had detention before.

"My mom's gonna freak," I whispered nervously.

"Good luck with that," he answered, his face going pale.

"It might be all right. But only because it's you."

He grinned his characteristic sideways grin, so full of charm, so full of crap. I never could understand what my mother saw in him. Always strictly polite to his elders, laying it on thick with the ma'ams and sirs that had already gone out of fashion, he was arguably the biggest troublemaker of all of my friends, and definitely the one most likely to try to get me naked. Yet he was the only one she'd still let into the house. Would even leave me alone with him in the bedroom, staying tactfully away from the open door. Almost as if she wanted something to happen.

I gave it to her straight as soon as we emerged from the classroom, before Josh, in spite of his valiant attempt to breeze briskly down the hall with all of the craft and subtlety of one of his

LORI SCHAFER

paper rockets, had even managed to escape from her sight. "Josh and I were fooling around in class and got detention. I have to come back after school."

Her lips twitched. I could see the internal conflict boiling within her, picture her cheeks reddening under her makeup as we tiptoed through the crowded corridor, drawing furtive glances from curious students. I didn't blame them for staring. It wasn't every day you witnessed an otherwise normal teen-aged girl being escorted to class by a conspicuous and over-dressed middle-aged woman. Kids I didn't know would pounce on me in the bathroom, nearly dissolving into hilarity at finding me for a moment alone and ripe for ribbing. "Aren't you the girl whose mother has green hair and comes to school with her?" they would snicker.

"It isn't really green," I would argue. "It's supposed to be blonde; something just went wrong during the coloring." It was more of a greenish tint than anything. The kind you get from swimming often in a chlorinated pool. Personally, I didn't think the hair looked anywhere near as stupid as the sunglasses. Wearing mirrored sunglasses indoors is surely not the way to avoid drawing attention to yourself when you're convinced that your ex-husband and adult daughter are stalking you.

My mother gritted her teeth, grinding them audibly as if literally chewing over the idea. "Then I guess we'll have to come back after school," she muttered bitterly, surrendering to painful necessity.

"Thanks. Otherwise I might get kicked out," I replied pointedly, hoping she'd catch the implicit threat of it. I'd already missed more than a month that quarter and could, according to school policy, be failed across the board purely on the basis of unexcused absences.

Someone had noticed, taken pity on me. Was it one of the string of psychiatrists my mother had sent me to, each of whom I had at length convinced that I was not the one who was crazy? Was it one of my teachers, someone who understood that honors students don't suddenly stop showing up to school for no reason? Was it my guidance counselor, who had been in the office the day my mother had tried to force me to sign the papers saying I was dropping out?

They'd made arrangements, the school board had informed her officiously. One of the teachers – the English teacher I'd had freshman year – had volunteered to take me in, and if she didn't let me come back, they would force the issue. I'd been truly touched. I

2

barely remembered Mrs. Silverman; recalled more vividly the handsome, witty boy who'd sat next to me during her class and who had eventually become my first boyfriend. I wondered what it would be like to live with her, her and the other troubled student she'd allegedly taken under her wing. Who would even have imagined that a small, close-knit suburb could hold two such students?

Even my mother, so bold in the face of imaginary enemies, was unwilling to risk official intervention. She'd let me come back. With conditions. I can't begin to guess what she told the principal and the superintendent – whether she in fact convinced them that I might be in some sort of danger, or if they merely thought it best not to chance it, never suspecting that the woman to whom they had admitted entrance was more dangerous by far than any of the nonexistent murderers she feared. But they had permitted it, this insane adult intrusion into the lives of unwitting high school students. As long as she stayed outside the classroom, not in it. Inside, they'd insisted, would be too distracting. But as a goodwill gesture they had commandeered for her a set of her own chairs, one parked outside of each of my classrooms, that she might not grow weary during her dull and lonely vigils. What kind consideration, I'd thought bemusedly. How nice that they'd made an effort to ensure her comfort.

"We're going home now," she announced. "You can skip P.E."

"I still have to come back for detention, Mom," I reminded her.

"I want to go home for lunch," she insisted, grabbing me awkwardly by the elbow while I slipped my book-bag over my shoulders.

I didn't argue. I succumbed to her clutch and followed her silently, listening to the swish of her floor-length skirt as we traversed the corridor towards the parking lot where the student vehicles were stored. Along the way, we spotted the vice-principal, a friendly-faced giant of a man, striding towards us. I nearly forgot myself and smiled. Following my first string of poorly explained absences, he had tried to be kind to me.

"Schafe!" he'd exclaim when he passed me in the hall, punching me gently on the shoulder with his beefy fist.

"Huff!" I'd answer back, grinning, with the kind of liberty in which only kids who were sorely pitied could safely indulge.

But that was before this, before I'd had a permanent, round-the-clock guardian. Now he didn't speak; barely even glanced at us as he edged cautiously away, retreating as far as possible against the wall, afraid to come too close to me or my mother. Backing away the way everyone did. I didn't blame them for that, either. They were right to do it.

We reached the double-doors that opened onto the parking lot, barred gates of freedom before which I would have cowed had I been alone. But she approached them boldly, as if it were her inalienable right to pass unhampered through the forbidden exit. It was a closed campus, but the hall monitors stepped politely aside to let us by as they always did, even if they didn't know about us. Parent with child. Free pass; no questions asked. Submission to parental authority was automatic, guaranteed. Indisputable.

An overcast sky was gradually divesting itself of lukewarm spring rain, sending tiny rivulets of rainwater along the curves of my skull and down the back of my neck like the tickling tendrils of unseen vines. I'd cast the hood of my raincoat aside, as I always did now. I didn't like the way it restricted my peripheral vision. Our windshield was spattered thickly with raindrops, but she didn't turn on the wipers; drove instead in half-invisibility, whether in an effort to conceal or be concealed, I couldn't say. She had covered her badly transformed hair with a plastic rain-bonnet, of an old-fashioned design I'd never seen before and haven't seen since. It reminded me of the handkerchief with which she'd attempted to cover up her previously dark, long, wavy hair that night we'd run away from the house some weeks before, shortly before my stepfather, utterly bewildered at the sudden turn of events, had agreed to move out. It hadn't done much to alter her appearance. I was noting carefully now the effectiveness of her various disguises. Preparing myself for when I needed one.

She fixed us sandwiches, grilled cheese and tomato, the butter-browned bread and melted cheddar infusing our kitchen with a near-heavenly scent. I hesitated before biting into mine, unsure if the meal would be suddenly snatched away, as my breakfast had been, on suspicion of it being poisoned while her back was turned. And unsure also, if one of these days it would be she who had done the poisoning. But she sat down and ate with me, apparently satisfied with the attentiveness of her own preparation, and I took that to mean that my lunch was safe. I wondered whether my dinner would be.

At two-thirty I packed up my homework and reminded her that we needed to go. "In a minute," she said vaguely, sitting taut and erect on the sofa in the hip-hugging jeans she'd changed into and snapping briskly through the pages of a woman's magazine. By a quarter to three I was nervous.

"We're going to be late," I said.

"We're not going," she yawned with affected nonchalance, rising casually from her seat to check the lock on the front door.

"I have to go, Mom." I spoke with the calm, measured tones I always used with her now, but inside I was panicking. "I can't let Josh sit for detention by himself."

Even the mention of her favorite didn't move her. "Then you shouldn't have gotten detention," she answered blithely, nodding to herself in undoubting affirmation.

I inhaled so sharply that my lungs burned with the force of it. Rose slowly from the table where I'd been studying. Deliberately donned my lavender raincoat, my hands shaking, sweat forming along my hairline like condensation over a steaming pot. Chose my words carefully, not wanting to suggest more than I meant.

"I am going to school."

I nudged past her to the door, placed my hand on the knob, and gave it a yank. She yanked back, all of her considerable might concentrated on the bones of my wrists, dislodging my grip from the door and sending me crashing through the sheetrock, leaving a nearly woman-sized hole in the wall.

"What do you want from me?!" she yelled nonsensically, as if I were a disobedient child having a fit of temper.

"I want my life back!" I shouted, conscious of the melodrama of it, my pathetic cry, but aware, too, that there was no elegant way to express what I wanted. And no hope of making her understand it even if I found the words with which to explain it.

She didn't answer, but swung me forcibly around again, causing me to hit the opposite wall of the foyer sideways, leaving a smaller, skinnier trench in the sheetrock. And then grabbed me by one hand, dragged me out to the car, and threw me inside as if I were an uncooperative luggage bag that had been carefully packed but still refused to clamp shut.

I swallowed, rubbing my wrist, relief flowing through me like the midsummer rainshower that so briefly releases the nearly constant tension of northeastern summer skies. I could still make an appearance at detention, might still be able to graduate on time and get out of this hellhole once and for all. She backed blindly out of the driveway and took off, far faster than usual. But not in the direction of my school. Towards the border, the state line.

"I could take you away," she'd told me once, smugly, after the first time I'd made a break for it and had to be hauled forcibly home. "Take you right into this airport and fly you anywhere I want to; somewhere no one will ever find you. And I am your mother and there is absolutely nothing that anyone could do to stop me." She'd smiled complacently as we drove around and around Bradley International Airport, humming cheerfully under her breath as she showed me the planes. Pleased with her cleverness, the infallibility of her plan, her power.

I held hard to my seat and harder to my fear. I focused on it, drew strength from it. I didn't speak. In silence I awaited an opportunity, a happenstance, a careless moment, while she screeched around wet, sandy curves, slamming me sideways, partly restrained by the seatbelt that was intended to ensure my safety but which was hemming me in, trapping me in the car with her like a circus animal in a travelling cage.

"You want a life?" she snarled unexpectedly as we approached a glaring red stop sign, barely tapping the brakes. "I'll kill us both!"

But my left hand was already on the latch of the belt strapping me into the vehicle; my right hovered by the door handle. I felt her fingers snatching at the vinyl of my jacket as I jumped and rolled uncontrollably out onto the pavement. I heard her cursing violently behind me as the car shuddered to a noisy halt. The backyard backwoods of New England sprawled out before me and I sprinted into them, clawed my way through branches and brambles and pricker-bushes, and came at last to a tall cyclone fence that I climbed awkwardly, my full-grown feet too large for its twisted footholds, and then jumped, catching my jeans on its pointed peak and tearing them nearly the length of the seam, scraping bits of the soft flesh underneath.

I stopped. Listened. No sound of pursuit came to my ears. I stopped breathing. Listened again. Scanned the sky and tried to judge my direction from the clouds hiding the sun. Took a tentative step, my footfall crackling the underbrush. Listened again and heard nothing. Looked and saw nothing, nothing but trees and bushes and pine needles and the slivered remnants of last autumn's leaves finally freed from the cover of snow.

And then began trudging the miles through the woods back to town.

I didn't make it to detention. I covered my ripped pants with my jacket and dragged my torn, tired body back through the deserted hallways of the school, leaving dirty footprints on the freshly polished floors and fingerprints on the classroom doorknob that rattled uselessly in my battered hands. Josh told me later that Mr. Cooper hadn't shown up, either. Apparently he'd forgotten all about assigning us detention. Had viewed it, perhaps, as a temporary, meaningless distraction from an important lesson in physics.

THE OBITUARY

MY MOTHER PASSED away in Florida on March 18, 2007, at the age of sixty. The owner of a local restaurant, she is survived by her final former husband and three daughters: April Schafer of Massachusetts, Sandra Johnson of New Hampshire, and Lori Schafer of California.

I found her obituary online in May of 2013. I was actually doing a search for myself. I've long made a habit of periodically checking the internet in order to see how much personal information is publicly available about me. Is it strange that I would do that? You'd do it, too, if you were me. You would want to know how easily you could be found.

I did stop, after a while. Looking over my shoulder, I mean. It wasn't because I ever stopped being afraid, ever stopped believing she might still come after me. But you learn to live with that kind of fear, even to disregard it. In recent years it's only hit me at odd moments and intervals, like when I suddenly remember her birthday, or pick up an old book I once saw her reading, or catch myself crying at Christmas, as she used to do. Or when I glance in the mirror and realize that I'm nearly as old now as she was the last time I saw her, almost a quarter of a century ago. We still don't look very much alike, the former she and the current I. I didn't inherit her majestic, slender but curvy frame, her golden complexion, or her lovely, soft hair, draped in long loose curls about her high-cheekboned face. All I got were her bad feet, her arthritic hands, and the perpetual dark circles under my eyes.

I haven't minded it much, not having her beauty. I don't think I'd like seeing her staring back at me every morning out of that relentless mirror, like some ghost from my teenage years that will never stop haunting me. It's only when I hear a recording of my own voice that I'm forcibly reminded that there is at least one part of her in me, the part that speaks. How I almost laugh when I remember how she used to answer the phone and pretend to be me when my friends called the house, how much information she got that way before people caught on that our voices were virtually identical. I didn't blame them. How could they have guessed? Their parents were only crazy in the usual ways.

My mother wrote to me in 2006, not long before she died. I wonder now if she knew she was dying, if she had been diagnosed with some terminal illness and this was her way of reaching out one last time. There was nothing about that in the letter, though. It went on about how well she was doing and how pleased she was with the new man in her life and she enclosed a newspaper clipping about the restaurant she owned now, just like she'd always wanted.

It was a very nice letter. She sounded happy.

How could she be happy?

I should have been angry; I should have been indignant at her gall in daring to address me as if I were merely a long-lost daughter whom she still dearly loved. I should have been stunned by her refusal to acknowledge that the break between us was anything more than teenage rebellion. I should have been horrified that she was still walking the streets, she, the formidable Judy Green-Hair — as she was known around town — a danger to herself and others. That after all these years she still felt no need to extend comfort, to offer assurance that she'd gotten better, to give confirmation that what she'd experienced had been no more than a temporary psychotic break and that she was sorry, oh, so sorry for what she'd made me suffer.

I wasn't any of those things.

When Mom first lost her marbles, I spent a lot of time trying to explain the things she said and did to other people. Oftentimes they wouldn't believe me.

"But why would she do that?" they would argue. "It makes no sense!"

No, it made no sense. Why would the same woman fight like a cornered beast to protect me one moment, then threaten to murder me the next? But it's a mistake to try to evaluate the behavior of the severely mentally ill by the standards of rational people. I'm sure in their own minds their behavior is perfectly rational. Perhaps in some ways it is.

It is almost logical when you consider it objectively. Of course she never felt any remorse over what she had done to me, her own daughter. She did what any decent mother would have done: she did what she thought was best for her child, she did what she thought was right. I don't believe my mother ever understood that she had anything to regret.

I spent the first seventeen years of my life with my mother. She spent her last seventeen years without me. A whole other lifetime, to a teenage girl. How I've wondered how much it hurt her when I left. How lonely she must have been. How she must have suffered. How she must have cried over losing us, all three of her daughters. A poor way for an old woman's life to end. A poor way, too, for a young woman's life to begin.

Perhaps one day I might have been persuaded to see her again. I haven't ever forgotten her, that other woman I once knew as Mom. Mom, the caring, devoted mother who worked three jobs to support my sister and me, who nonetheless found time to bake and teach me to read and ride bikes with me. Mom, the tough, independent woman who, at forty-three and in less than perfect health, thought nothing of moving a thousand miles all on her own to start a new life and revive her long-abandoned career. But without a diagnosis, without evidence of treatment, without knowing whether her illness was permanent or manageable or whether I might still be in danger from her, I couldn't have guessed which one of them I would meet if I went to her – the woman who had been the succor of my childhood, or the one who had been the bane of my adolescence. I could not take that chance.

The chance is gone now. It's been gone, these last six years, without my even knowing it.

Why didn't anyone contact me when she died? Clearly she knew where I was. Maybe if someone had told me that she was dying, I could have gone to her. I could have offered her my forgiveness, if she wanted or needed it. It would have been a small thing for me to give, to put her spirit at rest. And perhaps we could at least have closed it, that last chapter of our mutual lives. Perhaps that would have been worth the brutal pain of a final encounter.

Except that it wouldn't have worked. I would not have believed it. A letter, a phone call; I would have thought it was a lie and a ploy, an overdue attempt to bring me back, brought about, perhaps, by a new snap in her psyche. Perhaps this time she would believe it was me and not my sister hiding in the crawlspace over her kitchen, lying in wait to kill her or her latest husband. Perhaps I would be the new danger that had to be destroyed. Perhaps this time she would be more successful in destroying it.

I will never know, now, exactly what sent her over the edge the first time, whether there was, in fact, a precipitating event, or if it had been simmering beneath the surface for years, threatening to boil over at the slightest increase in the heat fueling her subconscious.

I'll never know, too, what might have become of me, had I not had to live through it with her, by her side. How different my life might have been had it only begun two years later, or fifteen years earlier, instead of then, in the middle of my junior year, when I was old enough to understand what was happening to her. When I was still powerless to do anything about it.

She rests, in peace. Perhaps now I can, too.

MOVING IN, MOVING OUT, MOVING ON

SHE PICKED ME up at the bus stop after school, playfully tooting the horn of our tiny blue Chevette as if I wouldn't immediately have recognized it on sight. But I was surprised to find it sitting there on my usually solitary three o'clock corner because it was only raining lightly, and even a downpour didn't usually divert my mother from her customary position that sogginess was good for the soul. I never minded anyway; I liked walking in the rain.

She didn't take me home, however. Drove right by our warm, dry house and brought me to the Abdow's Big Boy at the state line instead; ordered me a luscious ice cream hot fudge cake, my favorite dessert from that day to this. Smiled cheerfully and asked about my day and told me about hers. There was less to tell now. She'd become a stay-at-home mom just as I'd grown into a teenager and didn't need much supervision anymore. I missed her tales of the crazy customers who had frequented the diner she'd managed; her days without work seemed to border on boring.

But I listened politely to her story about the drycleaner and the line at the supermarket while I devoured my rare treat and she looked on in envy, refusing even a bite, and refraining, for once, from asking me how much homework I had and whether there were any tests scheduled that week. And when I'd finished my cake and cola, she picked up the check the server had deposited upon the table and fidgeted with it, tapping its hard edge against the polished wood along with her polished nails.

"Chris is coming to live with us," she blurted abruptly.

"Okay," I responded, after the briefest of pauses.

"I know it's going to be a big change," she continued.

"It's okay," I said.

"You don't mind?"

I shrugged. What could I say? I felt bad for my young nephew, even if he was kind of a noisy pain in the butt. But what could you expect from a five-year-old? Especially one who had lived the way he had.

She'd confided the horror stories to me already. How she'd visited their apartment unannounced and found him locked in the closet, starved and saddled with his own filth. How my older sister had confessed that sometimes her boyfriend big Chris would beat him, smacking around his coincidental namesake because little Chris was half-black and big Chris' own kid wasn't. How my sister had gone back to working in the strip-club to support them and how my mom suspected she was doing drugs again. How she'd finally contacted Social Services and they'd gone to confirm the rumors and suspicions, how they'd taken my nephew away.

"What about his dad?" I wondered, finding it horrible and difficult to believe that the unfortunate child was an outcast to both his parents.

"Kevin is not a fit father," she answered darkly, furrowing her brow as if warding off some mental image I was too young or world-unwise to see. "He'll be better off with us."

I nodded my comprehension. Kevin had never been exactly welcome in our home, and I assumed she knew things about him that I didn't know. I'd only seen him once, when I was about nine and had barged into my sister's room after school and found them lying naked in layers on her narrow twin bed, the stark paleness of her skin contrasting sharply with his gleaming blackness. All I really knew was that my sister had loved him in spite of the outdated but still-lingering local assumption that whites should like and respect black people, but never date them.

"A woman from Social Services is coming to visit the house tomorrow. It's very important that they see that we can provide a good home environment for him." My mother ran her fingers through her curly dark hair, fluffing it out and then patting it down again, a nervous habit in which she only engaged when she was exceedingly stressed.

"Right," I replied reassuringly. "Don't worry; I'll be on my best behavior."

"You always are." She nearly smiled, then hesitated before

speaking again. "I had to make some changes to the house, to prepare for their visit."

I scrutinized her curiously. "What kind of changes?" It sounded strange. As a rule she kept the house in impeccable order. It was hardly ever necessary to clean up when company was coming.

"You'll see when we get home."

I didn't have to wonder long why she'd taken pains to prepare me. A few years earlier, we'd moved from a duplex in the city to a small ranch-style house in the suburbs. It had only two bedrooms, the perfect size now that my sister was out on her own. But today it had a third bedroom, the wide-open area next to the kitchen that served as the den, its sliding-glass doors leading directly to the backyard. And standing in it was my own full-sized bed.

At first I was confused. "Does Chris really need a bed that big?" I pondered aloud. Previously he'd always simply slept on a twin mattress laid out on the floor when he'd stayed over with us.

"That's your bed," my mother returned.

"I can see that," I said. It even had my fluffy down comforter, my peach floral sheets and pillowcases on it. "But what's it doing out here?"

"This is where you'll sleep from now on," she responded, jacking up her eyebrows as if I were being more dense than usual.

I might have gasped had I not been rendered breathless. A lump rose in my throat and I was nearly overwhelmed with the urge to cry, but I fought it. I didn't want to seem selfish. I was certainly not the only kid in the world who didn't have a private bedroom.

"You see, they'll expect him to have his own room," she explained.

My mind struggled to turn her position into a rational one and failed. How could they believe a living environment was suitable when the kindergartner had his own bedroom and the teenager slept practically in the hall? The kid didn't even like being alone; he was constantly tagging along after one of us when he was around. I was the one who needed space.

I was entirely unaccustomed to giving my usually sensible mother advice. I tried to convey it to her with gentle persuasion. "They might not like it, Mom. If they expect him to have his own room, won't they expect me to as well?"

"No," she asserted, averting her gaze and offering no further explanation for her illogical contention.

I paused, even more bewildered, and wondered how much she really knew about how the system worked. "They might," I prodded mildly. And then brightened with an idea. "Hey, why don't I move into the basement? You know, temporarily, until after they've approved you as guardian?" The basement was a bit dark, but well-finished. I'd spent days the previous summer assisting my stepfather with the painting and sheetrock. I wondered what he would think about the new arrangement when he returned from his business trip the following week.

"No," she said again, as if the matter wasn't up for debate.

I stared at her a moment, then turned away to examine the room. None of my things were there; only the bed and a solitary night-table with my alarm clock sitting on it, boldly blaring the minutes and hours in digital squares of fire-engine red. I bent down to peer under the bed and came up empty.

"Where's the rest of my stuff?" I inquired uncertainly. "Did you leave it in my – I mean, in Chris' room?" A five-year-old might wreak havoc with my books and cassettes and childhood stuffed animals.

"I packed it," she answered curtly. "Everything's out in the garage." She pointed towards the fireplace mantel. "I left you some clothes."

I turned and found a pair of jeans and a T-shirt. I laughed mirthlessly, incredulous at her uncharacteristic lack of foresight. The piled-up winter snow was still melting and she hadn't even left me a sweater. "I think I'm going to need more than that, Mom. I'll just go out to the garage and dig out a few things."

I hadn't taken two steps when I felt her grab me by the arm, roughly. It was unlike her to handle me so, and I halted mid-stride, thinking maybe she'd lost her balance and had latched onto me for support.

"No," she repeated, releasing me as if reluctant to do so. "You're not to touch those boxes."

Again I struggled to wrap my mind around it, her unreasonable denial. What was she afraid of? Did she think I would make a mess of the garage before Social Services came? I was not a child; I was sixteen, and tidy by both nature and nurture. Why prohibit me from handling my own stuff?

"How come?" I said, trying not to sound contrary. I'd never yet

15

been the rebellious type.

Her jaw twitched. "Because I said so," she shot back, as if she truly had forgotten that I was no longer a child. "Now go wash up for dinner."

I'd bathed just that morning, but I climbed into the shower anyway and tried to wash away the nagging fear that was still nibbling at the edges of my brain, a fear that was gradually replacing my distress over so abruptly and unexpectedly losing my room, my sanctuary, the place where I studied and read and giggled on the phone with my friends and made out with my boyfriends. It was too hard to think about, and I soon stopped.

After my shower I put on the clean clothes she'd left me, along with the blue-denim jacket I'd worn to school because it was growing chilly as twilight fell. Then I returned to the kitchen and jumped. A strange long-haired blonde woman was standing there facing me, confronting me with mirrored sunglasses, my very own favorite tie-dyed sweatshirt, and hip-hugging jeans like my mom always wore.

"What do you think?" she asked nervously, fiddling with her nails. "Do I look like your sister?"

Again I was speechless. How could a forty-one-year-old woman expect to look twenty-four, however she fixed her hair and her clothes? And why would she want to?

"I'm going to reject Chris when I go to pick him up tomorrow," she explained, as if for one moment that day she had understood what I was thinking. "Dressed like this, so he'll think I'm his mother. So he'll forget about her; hate her as much as she hates him."

I couldn't answer. This plan sounded even more ludicrous than the bedroom reorganization, but equally pointless to argue about. I took my plate of pasta and ate it silently while she examined her reflection in the hall mirror, screwing up her face as if practicing a pose.

After dinner I washed and dried the dishes as I always did and planned my next move, my next attempt to work around my strangely altered circumstances. I had something important to do that evening.

My mother reemerged from the bathroom. She'd changed out of my clothes and the blonde wig and sunglasses and looked more or less like herself again. Except that she wouldn't quite meet my eye when I spoke to her.

I cleared my throat. "I know you don't want me making a mess in the garage, Mom. But you packed up my notes for my English term paper. It's due in two weeks. I really, really need them."

"I don't want you going out there," she insisted.

"I don't have to," I responded quickly, having already anticipated this potential objection, as nonsensical as it seemed. "They're in the drawer of my desk; you can go and get them for me if you want." She'd moved the furniture out, too. I'd peeked while she was changing.

She hesitated and appeared to consider it.

"No," she finally responded, with the firmness of considered conviction. "You'll just have to do without them."

And late that night, when I tiptoed softly from my new bedroom and out to the garage, flicked on the light and soundlessly retrieved the packet of three-by-five cards that contained my notes, the notes I was inexplicably forbidden to have, the absurdity of it struck me with full force, and suddenly I knew that something was really, really wrong. Something that had nothing to do with my nephew or my sister or Social Services, something that had to do with Mom and Mom alone.

And so I was somewhat relieved when Social Services came a few days later and returned my nephew to his father, who, it turned out, did want him and had been furiously fighting my mother for custody. And I wasn't too surprised when my mother advised me the following week that I needn't fret over that term paper because I wasn't going back to school anymore anyway. My biological father, it seemed, who'd offered little resistance to being kicked out ten years before and hadn't been heard from since, was lying there in wait to murder me, much as my sister was now lurking in the insulated crawlspace we called an attic awaiting her own chance for revenge. And when my mother removed me from my reclaimed room again a month later, and moved me in with her instead so that she might protect me round-the-clock from these unseen enemies, I hardly even balked, I was so well-prepared by then for such bizarre and unexpected turns of events.

My things remained in the garage, but it was much harder to sneak out there while she lay awake on the other side of that king-sized waterbed, waiting for me to make a move, any move that would take me away from her. But sometimes I did: while she was in the bathroom, the shower, the basement. Began shifting it slowly, gradually, undetectably into organized piles. Stuff I really, really needed, and stuff I didn't. Stuff I would a year later pack into the back of a station wagon and drive away with, and stuff I would leave behind along with my mother's increasingly impenetrable insanity. Things that were easily abandoned and forgotten. And memories that weren't.

BEFORE THE SICKNESS

JUDITH MARY TOCCHIO was born on February 25, 1947, in a small town in the Berkshires called Pittsfield, which, according to my mother, was an apt name for a poor community in which her family was poorer than most. I know very little about my mother's family. She had an older brother, my Uncle Ernie, whom we visited once or twice a year until he moved to New Hampshire when I was about middle-school age, and a younger sister, of whom we saw so little that I've long since forgotten her name. Her parents both passed away either before I was born or before I was old enough to remember them. She never spoke of them much, and I couldn't even tell you their names, what they died of, or what they did for a living. My impression was that her relationship with them was not the soundest, or the most loving.

I don't know very much about her early life, either. I only recall two events from her childhood. The first concerned kids teasing her over the pronunciation of her Italian name. "Are you Japanese, Judy? Is that why your name is Tok-y-o?" The second is of her family's house burning down, which she mentioned to me times without going into levels of detail that might have been disturbing for a young listener. While no one was hurt, this was understandably traumatic for her, although now I'm unsure whether this was due to the terror of discovering that the house was on fire, or the more practical horror of her already poor family losing all of its worldly possessions.

Poverty was the recurring theme of her youth. Whatever her parents did for money, it wasn't enough. They weren't in danger of starving, but they lived on the "poor side" of town, and, what was perhaps worst for my mother, the children were forced to wear hand-me-down clothes. This was more embarrassing for her than it was for her brother and sister because by the age of twelve or thirteen, she had already developed into a double-D cup and was daily humiliated by having to attend school with her large breasts squeezed into sweaters that were far too tight to contain them.

I know somewhat more about her teen years, but this information, too, is scattered and sparse. Again, only two events stick out in my mind. The first was when she quit school at the age of sixteen. Her reason? She couldn't stand learning typing! It surprised me to hear this, because my mother had always been so keen on me getting a good education, but in her youth, she perceived school as no more than a way to fill her days.

"The only options for work for a young woman in that place at that time," she told me, "Were to become a waitress or a secretary. And it was pretty obvious I wouldn't make a good secretary!"

There was a third option, of course, one that women had been pursuing for countless generations – that of becoming a wife and mother. She accomplished one of these at the age of eighteen, when my sister April was born. But this was entirely accidental, according to her.

"We did not have sex," she always insisted. "I didn't know I could get pregnant by heavy petting."

It's up for debate whether she actually married the father – a Ray something or other – because at times she told me conflicting stories. On one point she was firm – he went to prison before my sister was born, and when or if he got out, he was never heard from again.

My mother was always proud of being Catholic, but it was around this time that her practice of her faith lapsed. She claimed that the cause was a moral objection to some instance of local tithing, but I find it telling that her refusal to attend church anymore happened to coincide with her becoming an unwed mother, which was, of course, a much bigger issue for her generation. While she encouraged us to read The Bible, and taught us to say our prayers, my sister and I were not raised in any particular faith, and my mother did not attend church services again until the time of her sickness.

I don't know exactly what my mother did after having my sister. I know that she moved down to Florida for a while, where her grandfather lived. She was mainly employed as a waitress, and even occasionally as a lounge singer. She had a nice voice: deep, smooth, and pleasant to listen to, and she probably would have done well with formal training. She often sang along with her 8-track tapes, or with the radio, a habit I also adopted at an early age. She returned to Massachusetts before I was born, some seven plus years after my sister, and some time in the interim married my biological father, Karl Schafer.

He, too, is somewhat of a mystery; all I know about him is what my mother told me. The son of German immigrants in the post-World War II era, he had lost an ankle in the Vietnam War and consequently walked with a limp. He worked as a "presser," whatever that meant – I got the impression it was in an industrial dry-cleaning facility of some sort – and evidently was, or became, a horrible drunk. I have no recollection of that, although one of my few memories of him is of being brought to his regular bar.

He seems to have been a good enough guy when he wasn't drinking, but one day when I was maybe four or five, he reportedly pushed my mother down the stairs in an alcohol-fueled rage. She immediately became fearful of him and of what he might do, either to her, or to me and my sister. My mother was not the sort of woman to wait and see when it came to our safety, so she kicked him out of the apartment and, except for one brief return visit when I was six, he was never a part of our lives again.

He doesn't seem to have been terribly interested in being a father, not to me, or, evidently, to his other offspring. My mother once intimated that I had other half-brothers and sisters with whom my father was not involved, so I don't think I was the only scattered seed that had been cast off by the fathering tree. This was confirmed when I recently did some poking around online and discovered that my father had died in 2015. A comment posted on his obituary by a "Karl Jr." expressed the son's wish that he had gotten to know his father better. My guess is that he didn't particularly want to be known.

Karl was not my mother's first husband, nor would he be her last. I was fourteen or fifteen when my mother really began to talk to me – not as a parent speaks to a child, but as an older person speaks to a much younger friend. It was then that I learned some of the family secrets, including the rundown of all of the men in my mother's life, of many of whom I had been ignorant up until then. After my sister's father, she had married another man, a Charles K., but their marriage was annulled for reasons she never cared to explain. After my father, she married – and this came as a surprise – his brother, whom I had known only as my Uncle Mike. All I remember about him is his name and the fact that he was a pilot and wasn't around very much. That marriage apparently only lasted six months, and again, although my mother never told me what happened, the look on her face when she made the revelation suggested that it didn't end well.

I was entirely ignorant of all of this. My childhood, by and large, was a happy one, and I recall it with the cheerful nostalgia of any adult who was fond of her youth. I remember playing games outside with my friends, and swinging my Muppets lunchbox on my way to school, and splashing about in mud puddles when it was spring. I remember learning to ride my first bike, and how excited I was when we acquired a swingset for our backyard, and what fun we had playing hide-and-seek when the grass grew tall enough to cover our heads. I remember those wonderful Christmas Eves and Christmas mornings, with all of the packages stuffed under the tree, and the pretty colored lights blinking away the darkness of those cold, snowy nights. I remember sledding, and snow forts, and the crunch of autumn leaves beneath my young feet. I loved growing up in New England, and in spite of everything, I still carry a torch in my heart for Springfield and Longmeadow and for Massachusetts.

For my mother, however, the years without a husband were one ceaseless struggle. She was singlehandedly raising two kids on her own without even a high school diploma. Although she had other jobs – I remember she worked as some kind of unlicensed caregiver or nurse for a while – choosing a career in waitressing seems to have served her amazingly well. She had a surefire way of landing a job. "Volunteer to work a shift for free," she advised me. "Let the manager see what you can do." Of course, you can't do that nowadays – the human resources and worker's compensation people would have panic attacks – but as a means of getting hired, it was creative, clever, and highly successful. She made good money, and worked mostly at night, which was convenient because I went to bed early and my sister was old enough, if barely, to handle emergencies. She probably felt Mom's absence much more than I did, but she was probably also more keenly aware of the trials of being poor than I ever was. I don't really recall the years when my mother was working several jobs and feeding us from a giant pot of spaghetti that she made once a week, but my sister did. Perhaps she wasn't the most enthusiastic babysitter a little kid ever had, but she did it, and that made the difference in making my mother's livelihood sustainable for us.

I don't remember this level of poverty, although my mother assured me that it was sometimes severe. I don't remember the dilapidation of our apartment, the second floor of a rundown three-family home, only the joy of having a yard to share with the other tenants. If my room was small and a bit dark, at least it was mine, unlike that of my best friend, who was stuffed into one bedroom with her two older sisters. I don't remember the Christmas when my mother was panicking because she only had twenty-five dollars to spend on our presents, because all I wanted were pretty packages under the tree to look at and open; I never really cared what was in them. I certainly don't remember being malnourished or hungry, although the cause of my lifelong distaste for pasta may have been all those pots of spaghetti. I don't even remember my mother being gone all those nights she was working at her various jobs; indeed, in my mind, she was ever-present. I thought that our life together was full of activity, and full of leisure. There were trips to the playground, and trips to the lake, trips to the Catskill Game Farm in summer and to the Christmas Tree Shop in the Berkshires in winter. We spent many a sunny Sunday feeding the ducks in Forest Park, and many a snowy Saturday building snowmen on the front lawn. She helped me to make dioramas, dolls, and other crafts from ready-made kits, and yes, she even baked cookies just like a storybook mother.

My mother always said she wanted me to be her best friend, and in many ways, I was. She didn't always want me around – as an adult, now I recognize her subtle methods of getting time to herself – but we were together quite often, and it was enjoyable for both of us. With my sister being so much older and keeping mostly to herself, I was almost like an only child, and had as much attention as I could ever have wanted. This may have been reflected in my good behavior; in fact, I was so well-behaved that my mother's only consistent complaint was that I spent too much time reading.

"Stop holing up in your room like a mole and come watch TV with the rest of the family!" she'd exclaim.

I may have been the only kid in America whose parent told her to read less and watch more TV! But since I did not like to disappoint her, I agreed. I would take my books into the living room in the evening and, during the commercials, I would read.

But if my mother did not want me to spend too much time by myself, it was certainly not because she didn't want me to read. Her drive to educate me began very early; I arrived at kindergarten already knowing my numbers and letters and the rudiments of reading because my mother taught them to me. Her formal education had been so lacking that I quickly surpassed her in both mathematics and reading, but she never seemed to mind that her elementary-school-aged daughter had more academic skills than she had. In fact, she made a point of ensuring that, in spite of our limited funds, I had every academic advantage available to me. Thus she drove me downtown every week to meet with the school superintendent for special training in the brand new field of basic computer programming, and she quizzed me for practice when I was in the citywide spelling bee. And although I was dedicated and motivated when it came my classes, and never had to ask for help with my regular homework, Mom did make some brilliant suggestions in terms of my arts and crafts, and most notably for my seventh grade science fair project. It was to be a working model of the digestive system, and we built it together out of chicken wire and papier-maché, both the open torso and all of the internal organs. The coup de grace was the electric pump and plastic tubing she recommended I utilize in order to simulate the flow of substances in the course of digestion. That was probably what earned the project first prize.

It's so difficult even for me to picture the swift reversal that occurred in my mid-teens, and not only in terms of my mother's attitude towards my education. You might think, based on what happened later, that as a child I was subject to strict supervision, but that wasn't at all the case. The same woman who, when I was sixteen, snatched me from school, forced me to sleep in the same bed with her, and monitored my every intake of drink and of food, had permitted me to roam freely about our neighborhood from a very young age, just like all of the other blue-collar kids on our end of the city. As a child, I walked to and from school by myself; as a teen I was not even allowed to take the school bus. As a kindergartner, I could go as far as I wanted, as long as I was within hearing range of the shrill tongue-whistle that would summon me home, while as a junior, I always had to be where my mother could see me. In elementary school, I was allowed to travel to the library by bike, and could spend all day reading in the park or riding around picking up bottles and cans for pocket money as long as I was home before dark; in the latter part of high school, I was not even permitted to have a bike, and the money I earned was no longer my own.

Thus, as far as I can tell, my childhood contained no foreboding of my mother's illness. It's so tempting to reevaluate as we look back, so simple to find examples of possible mental instability or illness when we go looking for them. Yet all of us have experienced bouts of unusual behavior, all of us have suffered moments of unfounded depression, all of us have quirks in our personal lives. It's only in hindsight, when we recast the past lives of the future mentally ill in our own minds, do we think we see a pattern, evidence that suggests to us that we should have known this was coming. But in my mother's case, even this evidence remains very sparse.

When I was eight, Mom married John, the man she had been dating, who became what I like to call my "main" stepfather. He's the one I remember, the only man I ever thought of as being something akin to a "Dad," and I called him that without reservation. April was not so agreeable. I don't know what kinds of experiences she'd had with the other men in Mom's life, but she never seemed overly thrilled about having yet another new dad. Of course, it may not have helped that she was fifteen by then, and he only twenty-two; he and my sister were closer in age than he and my mother!

Even if he was ten years my mother's junior, and in a different stage of his young life, there is no doubt in my mind that they loved each other. Not only was my mother much older, but she'd had a hysterectomy shortly after my birth, when the doctors were unable to stop the postnatal hemorrhaging. "God broke the mold after he made you," was the way she described it. My stepfather must have known that they could never have the children he wanted, and he married her anyway. On her part, it's tempting to think that, as a struggling single mother, she married him for the money, but somehow I don't think this was so. Although he did eventually go on to be very successful at his chosen career in electrical engineering, at the time they were married, he was fresh out of college, and she made more money waitressing three nights a week than he did full-time at his entry-level position! Besides, she was always impeccably independent, right to the end. Even in the midst of her illness, as soon as she realized that her marriage was over, she began making plans to go back to work, bad feet or no. She had never asked for child support from my own father, and I doubt she requested alimony from my stepfather, either. She told me she would be getting $40,000 as settlement for the equity in her half of our home in Longmeadow, and that was probably it. A good chunk of money, but hardly enough for a middle-aged woman with physical issues to live on for the rest of her life – certainly not when she thought she would still have a daughter in college to support.

No, I don't think that marrying John was about financial security, just as none of her previous marriages had ever been. Actually, I suspect that her decision to marry again may have had something to do with me. I remember coming home one day from the first grade and telling my mom about a discussion we'd had at school that day – what our fathers did for a living. I'd been the only kid in the class who did not have a dad, so I told them what my mom did instead. I clearly recall not being upset about this at the time – in fact, I remember feeling unique, even special that our family was different from everyone else's. But my mother's face when I told her the story – it was filled with such sadness. Did she think I was complaining about the absence of a father figure? I wasn't. But she was married again within a year nonetheless.

It was at my mother's wedding that I first became aware of how attractive she was. All brides are beautiful, of course, but in latter years, those photos served as a reminder that she was quite pretty when she was young. She had pleasant if fairly ordinary brown eyes, and a long nose, and her Mediterranean roots plainly showed in the naturally tan tone of her skin. She put makeup on every morning – even when she was sick – and when I got older, encouraged me to do the same, although she never complained when I couldn't be bothered. She dressed casually – most often in a sweater and Gloria Vanderbilt jeans, the only cut and style that would fit her ultra-long legs. She had this gorgeous head of flowing, almost mahogany-colored hair that I envied years before I even cared about hair. She slept with those spiky round wire curlers in it every night, and woke up uncomfortable but looking great. Her looks diminished considerably when she got sick and cut off her hair. But maybe by that point she didn't care.

She still battled constantly to maintain her big breasts. How clearly I remember those tiresome trips through countless department stores, searching for extra-strength bras that would fit both her budget and chest! She blamed her breasts for her ongoing back problems, and I was always disturbed on the few occasions when I saw her naked – the shoulder straps cut deep gouges into her skin that looked rather painful. Otherwise she was quite pleased with her form and figure, and justifiably so. She was tall – quite tall, in fact, five-nine and a half, and no, when asked, she never would round it down to five-nine. Even when she was hurting, she always held herself proud and erect. She liked being tall, and she liked being slim – at my last recollection, she weighed a hundred and sixty-five pounds, which, although not thin, was relatively trim for her age and her height. She struck you as solid but not overlarge, and it wasn't until I had to physically fight her that I realized what a difference her height and size made. At five foot six, I was the short one – my sister grew to five-eight – but rarely in my life have I ever felt small. Of course, maybe it's harder to see when it's your own mother. As a kid, you expect your parents to be taller than you, and mine always was.

Yes, she was a good-looking woman, and she had plenty of other qualities that men find attractive. She was friendly, outgoing, and easy to be with, an accomplished cook and a meticulous housekeeper. Sometimes I've wondered why, with all of her husbands, she never found one who was wealthy enough to have relieved her burdens and removed her cares. I guess that just wasn't her way.

I don't really know if my mother and stepfather were happy after they married. At the time, it certainly seemed to me that they were, but as an adult, I can see now that much of their lives in their early years together revolved around work. Although having two incomes must have eased the financial burden, my mother's wages carried our family in those first years. They both participated in maintaining the household and caring for the children – namely, me. Although I was a highly independent kid by then, and an avid reader who didn't need much entertaining, my stepfather often watched me in the evenings while my mother was working, teaching me chess, solving math puzzles with me, and taking me mini-golfing. April, I believe, mostly holed up in her room. I suppose I was too young for her ever to talk to, but I have to imagine the change was difficult for her, perhaps even painful. Not only did she have another new father, but we had moved to Connecticut just before she started high school to be closer to his new job. After a lifetime in Springfield – and much of it in the same neighborhood, even the same apartment – the transition must have hit her hard.

Even though we returned to Springfield after only one year in Connecticut, all the moves hit me hard, too. Although, even then, I liked having new rooms I could arrange and new environments I could explore, I was not so thrilled about changing schools. All together, I switched schools six times between kindergarten and seventh grade, and trying to make friends year after year proved exceedingly difficult for me. I was nerdy, quiet, and shy, and never did manage to develop the outgoing personality that children who relocate all the time are supposed to enjoy. At home I had the kids I'd grown up with, the neighborhood children, but it took me a long time to form relationships at school with the kids in my classes, mostly other nerds just like me. To complicate matters, by the fifth grade I had entered the local magnet program for gifted children and was taking a bus forty minutes cross town every day to attend school, which created a total separation of my school and home lives.

To her credit, my mother did her best to soften the effects of these transitions, and she did so voluntarily, and not in response to any griping from me. In general, I was not a complainer. Very rarely did I ask for things – Mom always had the hardest time picking out my Christmas and birthday presents – and expressing frustration over my situation or making demands of my mother were simply not in my nature. But somehow she always knew what I would want, or what would upset me, and while she rarely made decisions solely based on my needs, she did try her darnedest to make those decisions as easy on me as they could be. During the lonely year in Connecticut, for example, she brought me back to our old city a few times for afternoon visits. When we later moved to a different area of Springfield, she granted me permission to ride back and forth on my bike to our former neighborhood, a good half-hour each way, quite a long ride for a child of nine. A few years later, when we finally moved out to the suburbs when I was in the middle of the eighth grade, she drove me down a few times to see my old friends, and even brought my best friend back to the new house once so she could see where we lived. Most importantly, for the rest of the school year she drove me to the magnet school every day and picked me up, just so I wouldn't have to make that mid-year transition before starting high school. She was no longer working a regular job by then, but still, she did not have to do that. She also intervened on my behalf to stop one move entirely in my sophomore year. My stepfather had been offered a big promotion and nearly double the salary if he changed positions – but it would have necessitated relocating to the Midwest, specifically to Fort Wayne, in Indiana. I had never been overly thrilled about moving, but a change at this time would have been particularly devastating for me. I finally had a good group of friends at my new school, and I would, once again, be starting over, and in a place that was totally foreign to me. My mother sat me down to talk it over with me, to see how I would feel about making the move. Even by fifteen, I was incapable of throwing fits or complaining, but I did tell her that I did not want to leave, and next thing I knew, the matter had dropped, the decision had been made; we were not moving. I have to give my stepfather credit for this as well. Although he did still quickly advance through the ranks of his local firm, he took a big risk with his career for the sake of a kid who was not even his – and I don't even remember hearing them argue about it.

The summer before I started third grade, we left Connecticut and moved back to Springfield, to the same apartment we had left only the previous year – I guess no one else wanted it. But it was less than a year before we moved again, this time to our very first house.

This, in my mind, is when my mother truly began to reveal the central aspects of her personality as well as her special gifts. They bought the place for $33,000, which was a bargain even in the early eighties, and my mother took it upon herself to remodel and fix it. By then she had severely cut back on working – long years of waiting tables had taken their toll on her back and feet, and, at thirty-four, she simply wasn't up to that kind of repetitive physical challenge day after day. Eventually she would abandon waitressing all together, although she did occupy at least one restaurant management position, which gave her a host of skills and experience that would be invaluable to her when she opened her own place more than a decade later. But she was never the type to be idle, and since the reduced hours gave her plenty of extra free time, she invested all of it in that house.

Sometimes it's hard to imagine. This was the girl who had quit school because she lacked the drive and discipline to suffer through one course of typing, yet here she was at hard labor, spending hours every day cleaning and painting and planting bushes and flowers. The house was so cheap because it was a dump – and I mean that literally; it was strewn with garbage when we arrived. My mother re-did it all, from sanding the crud off of and refinishing the hardwood floors, to scraping the old peeling wallpaper off of the walls, she re-made that house from the bottom up. There were eight rooms, so not only did we all have our own bedrooms, but my stepfather even had his own office; plus it had walk-in closets and a large enclosed balcony that surveyed the street. Even after Mom's remodeling, the house was mysterious, and charmingly spooky; somehow it always reminded me of Nathaniel Hawthorne's House of the Seven Gables. Not only was it a great place, it proved to be a wise investment. It was what was called a Boston duplex; the house was three stories, with our half occupying half of the second and all of the third floor, leaving the other half available to rent. After she had finished fixing it up, my mother invited her best friend Nancy and her two children to move in to the lower unit for the same rent they had been paying at their old apartment. Their rent basically covered our mortgage, making it a good deal for everyone. Nancy eventually moved out, and my mother and stepfather sold the house after only three years for $96,000. This was enough to finance our move to the suburbs.

This, in essence, was who my mother was, who she'd always been. She worked hard, she made plans, and she thought things out. This was how she had managed to feed and house two young children all by herself; this was how she had managed to thrive without education. She had no credentials that demanded respect, but she had no trouble earning it, not from me or from anyone else who knew her well. She may not have been smart, and she may not have been educated, but she had a practical way of approaching the world that doesn't necessarily come to those with either smarts or education. I remember her telling me a story once about an incident involving her coffee shop:

"Management wants to raise the price of coffee from twenty-five cents to seventy-five cents. They keep telling us that higher prices will mean bigger tips from our customers, but I disagree. Most of the people who come into the shop only have one cup of coffee. When they're done, they leave a buck on the counter – twenty-five cents for the coffee, and seventy-five cents for the lady who poured it. Now what do you think is going to happen when they raise the price of coffee to seventy-five cents? Customers will still leave a buck on the counter, but now it will be seventy-five cents for the coffee, and twenty-five cents for the woman who served it. The store will be pocketing an extra fifty cents in change that used to belong to me."

Naturally, it panned out just as she'd predicted, and through all my years in accounting, this is a lesson I have never forgotten. The numbers do matter – but so do the practical aspects of human behavior. That was something my mother taught me, and she definitely didn't learn it in school. My mother may not have been gifted with a high level of intelligence, for which she might easily have compensated had she simply had more education. But she possessed great quantities of a quality that many academically-minded people lack – good sense. She was a very, very sensible woman. The kind of woman who knows how to make things happen. The kind of woman who could put together a plan and put it into action; the kind of woman who never sat back and waited to see what the world would bring her, but who leapt onto the field and tackled it head-on herself. This was what made her such an asset at work, at home, at whatever she attempted. Unfortunately, it's also what made her such a formidable opponent during her mental illness.

By the time we made the move to Longmeadow, it became astonishingly clear that all of this was a part of Mom's plan for our lives, and most of all, mine. Over the years she had become even more increasingly determined that I get a good education. Perhaps she'd had the same hopes for my sister, but if so, she had been disappointed. As my mother phrased it, April had "gotten good grades until she discovered boys," and when she became pregnant late in her junior year, it had become doubtful whether she would finish high school at all. Her son Chris was born while we were still in Springfield, and although she did graduate, and continue to live with us for a time, she moved out shortly after turning eighteen. It's unclear to me whether this was voluntary, or if she was asked to leave. In any case, my mother wasn't particularly interested in inviting her back. She told me later than one of the things she liked about the house in the suburbs was that it was too small for us ever to have to take in my sister and her growing baby!

But that wasn't the main motivation behind the move. I was twelve years old and in the eighth grade when my mother laid it out for me.

"We've sunk all of our money into this house," she informed me. "We won't be collecting rent here, and the mortgage and property taxes are high. But the school system is one of the best in the region, and we had to decide – did we want to save that money for your college, or spend it on your high school education?"

They had chosen the latter. Longmeadow High School was unarguably one of the best public schools in the state, and the difference could be felt the second you walked in through its front doors. The kids were smart, and competitive, and ten times more engaged than those at my junior high. Like me, they actually wanted to study, and wanted to learn, and it showed in both the scholastic awards and in the spectacular college acceptance and attendance records. There was no doubt that I was about to get a first-class education, but as my mother was quick to point out, there were downsides.

"You won't shine as much here as you would have if we'd stayed in Springfield, where there's less competition. You'll have to work even harder, and you'll need to, because we can't afford to send you to college. If you want to go, you'll need to win scholarships, so you'd better get cracking!"

Perhaps this was a lot of pressure to place on a child, but I didn't see it that way, and neither did my mother. In both of our minds, she was merely being practical, which was one of her greatest strengths. Besides, if she was going to say it at all, it had to be before I started high school; the warning would have been useless if she'd waited until I was too close to graduation.

In any case, I did not need to be warned. I had always excelled in school and saw no reason why I shouldn't excel here as well.

My mother didn't quite share my confidence, an opinion which she made clear in my first month at my new school, during which I brought home a (gasp!) B+ on my first Algebra II test.

This is the first time I remember ever truly being annoyed with my mother. It was also the first time I ever doubted her practicality or judgment. True, I had gotten a B+, which was a rare event. But I was also taking Algebra II as a freshman, which put me two years ahead of the regular track, which meant that I was in the same class with the advanced sophomores. In addition, I had been forced to sit and listen on Back to School night while my chauvinist new teacher informed a classroom full of parents that, in his experience, "Girls who have done well in math up to this point often find that they're no longer good at it." This was both infuriating to me as a budding feminist and insulting to me on a personal level, and there was really no way I was not going to do my darnedest to show that teacher up.

My mother did not seem to get that. She reacted to that B+ by lecturing me for literally two hours every day for the next month, which I found highly illogical. How was I supposed to study when her stupid lectures were taking up all of my time? Besides, never once in my life had she had to prod me into doing my schoolwork, and I found it incredibly irritating that she was taking such a hardened stance now, particularly when her lectures were actually preventing me from attaining our common goal. (Incidentally, I ended up acing that class, finishing with a 96 average, almost an A+. Take that, Mr. Giffin!)

But what's perhaps more significant here is not what she did, but how I responded. I sat through those boring, pointless, even counterproductive lectures – every last one of them. I did not argue, I did not walk away, I did not go to my room and slam the door like a lot of twelve- or thirteen-year-old kids would have done. I can't say I was always listening – those conversations got pretty repetitive – but I certainly did my best to pretend that I was, and to this day I don't know exactly why that is. I simply did not defy my mother. I would have thought it rude and ill-mannered to argue with her, and walking away from her while she was talking was completely out of the question.

As a child, I was not what you'd call a goody-goody. I got up to my fair share of mischief, and although I had always been a bad liar, I was quite capable of keeping secrets from Mom if I thought I had done something of which she might not approve. I had been warned, for example, not to go swimming in the Connecticut River because it was so polluted, but I saw no reason to object when my friends suggested standing in the water and fishing instead. I knew my mother wouldn't have liked me dumpster-diving with my treasure-hunting friends, so instead I stood outside the bin, keeping watch and organizing the plundered loot. I didn't tell her when I smashed into a car on my bike, or when I kissed a boy for the first, second or third time. I was not an automaton, obedient to her every whim, but I was no rebel, either. I didn't vandalize, didn't steal, didn't smoke; heck, I was fifteen before I said my first swear, and even then, the words felt funny coming out of my mouth, almost like Mom was right there, hearing me curse. I remember her telling me when I was a child that I shouldn't do anything I wouldn't do if she were around, and I suppose I took the admonition to heart. I was willing to throw a bend into her rules, but very rarely would I break them in two. It was this long-ingrained habit of obedience and complacence that made me vulnerable to my mother's insanity, and that also often saved me from incurring her violent wrath. In time I would have to rebel to save my own skin, but in the short-term there was much to be said for being good.

Even before she got sick, I knew that my mother was more rigid than other parents, that my curfew was earlier and more strictly enforced, and that, for example, I would never have been permitted to travel to France for Spring Break with the other kids in my class even if we could have afforded it. But this was hardly a sign of her illness. I was allowed to go out, allowed to have friends, and allowed to date boys. Her rules were not too tough or too overprotective; they were simply her rules, and for the most part, I obeyed them. When, in her mind, she invented all these infractions, when she imagined this litany of sins that I had committed, it only made the power of her delusions more frighteningly clear. I had spent my whole life trying not to upset her, even trying to please her, and her unjust accusations demonstrated how great was her loss of touch with reality, and with her own daughter. I was fortunate that I was good, fortunate that I was well-behaved and an A student, because of the leeway it bought me with my teachers and school when Mom got sick. But with my own mother, it bought me nothing; my lifetime of following her orders would come to naught.

The rest of my high school years – up until the time of her illness – were relatively uneventful. I became ever more immersed in schoolwork and in extra-curricular activities, and, although I didn't know it, undoubtedly became less and less involved with my mother. While my childhood and pre-teen years are filled with memories of time spent with Mom, I don't recall doing recreational things with her at all when I was a teen, except for our summer vacations at the North Shore and occasional air-conditioned afternoons at the movies. Still, she participated in my life in the ways you would imagine a good mother would. She routinely attended my concerts for choir and band, and even the plays in which I had bit parts. Although she didn't want me working during the school year, she approved of me getting jobs during the summers, and she arranged to drive me to and from work. Although she would later refuse to let me have a license, she did take me to Driver's Ed when I was old enough to get my permit, and brought me to the empty high school parking lot in her car on weekends to practice. She invited my girlfriends over for parties, and was friendly and polite to my boyfriends when I began dating. She continued to tolerate my impatience for shopping, but finally forced me to choose my own clothes, and she nudged me into changing the look I'd had since the first grade by suggesting a modern new hairstyle and by getting my ears pierced and buying me earrings. We'd already talked about the basics of sex, but she bought me a book to fill in the rest of the details, thus sparing us both the embarrassment of a conversation neither one of us really wanted to have.

What was she doing on her own all this time? I don't rightly know. Like most adolescents – and many adults, for that matter – I was almost entirely absorbed in my own life and didn't give much thought to what was going on with my mother. Sometimes she worked, but mostly she didn't, because her physical condition wouldn't permit it. She spent some time with her grandsons (there were now two), but April doesn't seem to have been overly fond of having her over, and I'm not sure she saw them as much as she would have liked. She cooked and kept house and took to more intensive reading. For as long as I could remember, there had always been a novel-in-progress on a shelf in our bathroom, but oftentimes now I would find her in a chaise-lounge in the backyard, her brow furrowed in concentration over some work of non-fiction. I remember how astonished I was to see her so enthused over one book she was reading: it was *The Fatal Shore*, by Robert Hughes, a comprehensive tome telling the story of Australia's founding. Her description of it was so compelling that when I ran across a copy a quarter of a century later, I took it home and read it myself.

I couldn't say whether by this time she and my stepfather were still happy, either. In my pre-teen and early teen years they had gone out once a week – I loved that because it meant I had the house to myself for a few hours – but their date nights seem to have diminished after a while. Honestly, I don't remember my stepfather being around all that much in my last years at school. He had received several raises and at least two promotions, but he worked longer hours and was away on week-long business trips probably half a dozen times every year. Without her friend Nancy, who had died of breast cancer recently, and without any other friends that I can think of, I can imagine now that my mother must have been very lonely. But if she was, she didn't complain, and I didn't notice.

Although I was unaware of it at the time, perhaps the most significant event of the pre-illness period transpired early on in my junior year, some months before she got sick. Since the beginning of the school year, I had been struggling. In addition to taking AP History, AP Physics, AP English, AP French, and AP Calculus, as well as the required Physical Education, I was singing in two choirs, playing clarinet in the wind ensemble (and occasionally the orchestra), and, at my insistence, had continued my summer job waiting tables on weekends. Although I was still doing fine in my classes, I was exhausted because I was not sleeping. Even worse, I quickly found that calculus, unlike algebra, geometry, or trigonometry, did not come naturally to me, and since my crazy schedule was only possible because my teacher and guidance counselor had both given permission for me to be excused from one class session per week, I had to work even harder to make up for the instruction I missed.

I don't know what triggered it, but one day in October, my mother informed me that in addition 855to quitting 8my job, she had decided that I should change my class schedule. She had contacted my school, an+d had arranged for me to switch out of AP History and AP Physics, and to drop out of the math class all together, which wouldn't be a problem since I was already so far ahead of track. Naturally, I was very upset, as much by her decision as by her interference. I reminded her that even if I did end up with a couple of Bs, they counted the same as As in regular track classes because they were APs. Furthermore, I would receive college credit for the Advanced Placement classes, which could save a fair amount of money on tuition when I applied to universities. In addition, changing my schedule now would mean that I would have to catch up on several weeks of work for the classes I'd missed; I would have homework and tests I would have to complete right away, albeit easier ones. Finally, as demanding as they were, I liked my classes, particularly AP History, which made U.S. history come alive for me in ways that other history classes had never done.

But she was insistent, and in any case, the request had already been made.

What could I do? I acquiesced, and obeyed; I went along, just as I had always done.

It must be incredibly difficult for people who know me now to imagine me being told what to do and actually doing it. I am not known for quiet acquiescence, or for going along with something with which I disagree because I'm not wired to disobey. But when it came to my mother, I never fought back; I did what she told me.

It turned out to be for the best. I would have flunked all of those classes when Mom took me out of school later that year. Even if those teachers had also been willing to overlook the seven unexcused absences rule (if you missed seven classes in a quarter, you automatically failed), I could never have kept up with the work on my own, particularly not when I wasn't allowed to do homework, and all of my textbooks were locked up in the garage. I would have failed junior year and changed the course of my life forever.

But I do have to wonder now whether this was the first observable sign – the earliest indication that something was going on with Mom's mind. All my life she had wanted me to do well in school, and in high school, especially, she'd really pushed me, so it made little sense for her to change that stance now. At the time I'd assumed that she was merely concerned about me, but in light of what happened just a few months later, I find myself considering the possibility that this sudden shift in her priorities had a more sinister origin. One minute she's rearranging my class schedule without my permission; the next she's dragging me down to the office, trying to force me to sign the papers saying I was quitting school all together. Surely such a swift reversal had to mean something.

What was particularly bizarre about it was that she had stepped in to a school situation on my behalf just a few weeks before. I had decided to try out for the math team. I had been on one in junior high, so I certainly had the interest and the experience. The teacher who led the team said that the members would be determined by the results of a test, with the six highest scorers being selected. When the results were announced, I had not been chosen. I was disappointed, but probably wouldn't have thought much about it except that my good friend George, who was a senior, had made the team – even though he had scored lower on the exam than I had.

Needless to say, I was extremely upset about this. I approached the teacher, thinking perhaps there had been some sort of (ironic) mathematical error. Failing that, I at least wanted some explanation for why I was being treated unfairly. Was he, too, part of the "girls-can't-do-math" club? Well, he refused to tell me anything, so I went straight home and shared the story with my mother, who had surprisingly little to say on the subject. The next day, however, unbeknownst to me, she went down to the school and raised hell with the principal and with that teacher. He finally informed her that he didn't want me on the team because I had been giggling with my friends before the exam about being on the math team and he was afraid I wouldn't take it seriously. At that point, it didn't matter, of course, because I couldn't very well have asked to replace George, and besides, I would still have an opportunity to be on the team when I was a senior. But I was incredibly impressed by how Mom had stuck up for me, and even though by then I was becoming increasingly assertive in addressing my own needs, I still appreciated having a supporting adult in my corner.

Was that what she thought she was doing when she changed my schedule – sticking up for me? Perhaps she really did think I was working too hard; perhaps she was afraid she had put too much pressure on me. But it seems very strange that in September she had tried to secure me a place on a competitive team, and by October she was lightening my workload without even consulting me. I had not changed, because I was still doing what I was told. But she had changed, and very soon I would have to change with her.

We had both set the stage for the next phase of our lives, she and I. My mother had always been my best friend, my ruler, my conscience, my guide. But the woman who confronted me that early spring morning when she took my room was no longer my mother. She would have to learn that she could starve me and beat me and even imprison me, but she could not control me. And I would have to learn that turning my back on a lifetime of obedience was the key – the only key – to my survival.

THE ILLNESS

LATE ONE EVENING a number of years ago, I was working in my home office and listening to a television crime show, one of those documentaries that delves into the twisted minds of men and women who have committed terrible atrocities. I heard a woman speaking. She was making, gravely and with utter sincerity, some of the wildest accusations you have ever heard. She had killed her new roommate, she explained, because the roommate had actually been sent to her home by some government secret agent in order to dispose of her, the murderess. So naturally she'd had to eliminate the roommate first.

I stopped working and looked at the TV. The woman's name was Diane. I didn't recognize her, but there was something compelling, almost familiar about the tone of her voice. At the interviewer's instigation, she began to present evidence – reams of explanation and corroboration – to establish the truth of her claim. She was unbelievably convincing. I hadn't the slightest doubt that she firmly believed every word she was saying. And indeed, provided you accepted the unlikely premise that the government was out to assassinate some obscure middle-aged woman for some even more obscure conspiratorial cause, every other aspect of her argument made perfect sense.

She reminded me so much of my mother that I got up and walked over to the TV to see if maybe it was her, after all.

As far as I know, Mom's mental illness was never diagnosed. To this day, I don't know what she had. Schizophrenia, everyone said, which is, of course, the best known of the psychotic disorders, affecting approximately one percent of the population[1], and a very strong possibility for the condition that afflicted my mother. Would she have been diagnosed with it had she ever sought treatment? It's probable. Further investigation would have revealed whether she met the criteria listed in the *Diagnostic and Statistical Manual of Mental Disorders*, the definitive psychiatric guide to diagnosis and treatment.[2] Briefly, the guide specifies the following signs and symptoms:

1. Symptoms of illness have been present for at least six months.

2. There has been deterioration of functioning from previous levels in such areas as work skills, social relations, and self-care.

3. Symptoms do not suggest organic mental disorders or retardation.

4. Symptoms do not suggest manic-depressive illness (bipolar disorder).

5. Either a, b, or c must be present:

   a. Two of the following for a significant period of time and for at least a one-month period:

   - delusions
   - hallucinations
   - disorganized speech, such as frequent loose associations or incoherence
   - grossly disorganized or catatonic behavior
   - negative symptoms, such as emotional flattening or apathy

   b. Bizarre delusions that other people in the individual's culture regard as totally implausible, such as the belief that thoughts are being taken out of the person's head and broadcast over the radio.

   c. Prominent auditory hallucinations consisting of voices keeping up a running commentary on a person's behavior, or two or more voices conversing with each other.[3]

Other factors might support this diagnosis as well. Many schizophrenics do experience cycles of relapse and remission, which could potentially explain the long-term pattern of her behavior; some schizophrenics even suffer only single psychotic episodes, as my mother may have done.[4] On the other hand, schizophrenics are usually diagnosed in their late teens and early twenties; late-onset schizophrenia, occurring after the age of forty or forty-five, and most often in middle age, comprises only fifteen to twenty percent of all diagnosed cases.[5] In the United States, for example, three-quarters of those who get schizophrenia do so between the ages of 17 and 25; it is unusual for initial onset to occur before the age of 14 or after age 30.[6] Late-onset schizophrenia, however, is often characterized by symptoms similar to my mother's: compared with early-onset schizophrenia, it features more paranoid delusions, more visual, tactile, and olfactory (pertaining to smell) hallucinations, and fewer "negative" symptoms such as catatonia and thinking disorders.[7]

But schizophrenics of any age rarely recover all on their own, and aren't generally able to function well in society without treatment. This is why a third of the six hundred thousand homeless people in the United States have schizophrenia or bipolar disorder, and why a fifth of the two million prisoners in American jails have a mental illness, many of them incarcerated for minor crimes such as trespassing, a common infraction of schizophrenics.[8] Even with medication, which can help to manage the disease, the prognosis is not very promising, and untreated patients tend to fare poorly. Seldom do they pack up their things, move twelve hundred miles away from their home, marry their sixth husband, and open a diner without ever obtaining medical help.

The woman Diane that I saw on TV was not a schizophrenic. She had a type of psychosis – a mental condition in which a patient loses touch with reality – called a delusional disorder. This rare illness is characterized by a patient's unwavering belief in something that is obviously untrue, such as a conviction that someone is following them without there being any logical reason why anyone should do so.[9] Individuals suffering from this disorder may function fairly normally, only acting out in strange ways when confronted with the subject of their delusions, as with Diane and her woefully misguided attempt to defend herself against her roommate's planned assassination.[10]

And sometimes I wonder if this is what actually happened to my mother. Like schizophrenia, delusional disorder is typically a chronic or ongoing condition, but some people do recover completely, while others experience episodes of delusional beliefs alternating with lengthy periods of total remission.[11] I have often wondered how, after being so sick, my mother managed to resume a normal life and even flourish in spite of her illness; as far as I know, in the seventeen years after I left her and before she passed away, she was never treated, never hospitalized, never confined to an asylum. If she did recover, then it seems strange that she never seemed to realize that she had done anything odd, and if she had always had this mental illness, then why did I have an essentially normal childhood and terrible teen years? Could the mere fact of being removed from the source of her delusions ultimately have permitted her to get better?

No one will ever know, and it may not be relevant, in any case. Schizophrenia and related disorders are incredibly complex, and often defy singular diagnosis. Schizophrenia alone may appear in numerous different forms, including paranoid schizophrenia, which has as its central feature delusions of a persecutory nature; hebephrenic or "disorganized type" schizophrenia, which primarily involves disordered thinking; catatonic schizophrenia, which is characterized by behavioral disturbances such as rigidity and stupor; and so-called simple schizophrenia, which includes a loss of interest and initiative, withdrawal, blunting of emotions, and the absence of delusions or hallucinations.[12] Numerous other conditions which are diagnostically distinct share many features with schizophrenic disorders, including schizotypal and schizoid personality disorders, paranoid and borderline personality disorders, even schizoaffective and bipolar disorders, suggesting that such conditions exist along a spectrum of mental illness rather than as entirely separate diseases.[13] Even delusional disorder is widely believed to be a less developed form of schizophrenia, with sufferers having delusions that are untrue but not wholly unreasonable, and in which hallucinations are either absent or not a prominent feature.[14]

I could not say for sure whether my mother experienced hallucinations. Certainly the language she used to describe her delusions sometimes suggested she had: for instance, that she had seen my biological father standing on a sidewalk in our suburban town, that she had seen the list they kept at the police station of suspected Satanists. Other evidence to support her convictions was murkier, and less specific. She believed that my sister was hiding in the attic because she thought she had heard something in the tiny crawlspace over her head, and because once she had seen the garage window left open. If she had auditory hallucinations, as are so common with schizophrenia, she never mentioned them; never did I overhear her talking to herself or participating in conversations with invisible people or inaudible voices. Olfactory hallucinations and hallucinations of taste, however, could explain why she was so firmly convinced that her food was tainted or poisoned. This sometimes happens in patients with schizophrenia who suddenly find that familiar foods smell or taste "funny," and subsequently become convinced that someone has been tampering with their meals.[15] There is no doubt that she was paranoid, and believed very strongly in her own persecution, yet she demonstrated none of that disordered thinking common to many patients with schizophrenia; indeed, although the basis of her logic was lethally flawed, she proceeded to act with a cold rationality that made perfect sense in its own roundabout way. If you believe that you're being poisoned, then naturally you will not eat; if you believe that your daughter may be in danger, then of course you will keep her under lock and key.

Whatever the technical name for her condition, even modern medicine cannot determine what might have caused it. That schizophrenia tends to run in families has been known for at least two hundred years[16], yet sixty-three percent of people with the condition have no familial history of the disease.[17] Modern imaging techniques have shown that there are neurological defects and structural changes within the brains of schizophrenics, and there is abundant evidence that people raised in urban areas or born in the winter or spring are more likely to get the disease.[18] The effects of general psychological stresses are more open to debate, and even though I personally believe that schizophrenia is a biological illness, there was a time when I became willing to let myself doubt. In 2011, at the age of thirty-nine, right around the age when my mother sickened, I was diagnosed with arthritis. By 2013, it was excruciating, all-over-my-body arthritis, and by 2014 I was disabled, no longer able to work, travel, hold a glass or a pencil, or pick up a sheet of paper without pain that was unbelievable, and virtually unbearable.

After five years I discovered that I had been misdiagnosed; that the "arthritis" that had nearly ruined what was left of my life was nothing more than a deficiency of a common nutrient, iron; I relate the story at length in my forthcoming memoir *It's the Iron*.

But while I was sick and endlessly suffering, while I was enduring the anxiety and deep depression that iron deficiency can also cause, I often thought of my mother, and of her condition. She, too, had complained of arthritis in her hands and feet, although in my recollection, it was nothing like mine. But what about those mysterious foot operations she had to have later? What about the ongoing pain in her spine? Could she have suffered from this form of arthritis as well? Could I have inherited her physical illness?

Because if she did, and if I had, then suddenly I understood. Because being in that much constant pain could make you crazy; it was enough to make anyone crazy.

There's no way to know what truly triggered her illness, because the development of mental disorders is not well understood. Causes may be genetic, environmental, or some combination; quite likely there is no single cause. A variety of diseases and medical conditions, including brain tumors, multiple sclerosis, and head trauma, can induce psychotic symptoms; even some common medications can prompt delusions or hallucinations [19] Certain viruses are known to cause brain abnormalities and other dysfunction, and specific nutrient deficiencies – like my friend iron – can cause anxiety, depression, and other emotional symptoms. But schizophrenia, while it can have severe emotional consequences, is not in the class of mood disorders. Schizophrenia is a psychosis, a type of mental illness in which a person cannot distinguish what is real from what is imagined. [20] This can make patients irrational, unpredictable, and sometimes even violent.

My mother was somewhat unusual in that she became physically aggressive and outwardly violent, because in general, schizophrenics are more of a danger to themselves than to others. Suicide is the number one cause of premature death among schizophrenics, with ten to thirteen percent of sufferers killing themselves and as many as forty percent making the attempt. [21] On average, a schizophrenic patient is one hundred times more likely to kill him- or herself than somebody else. [22] But this is not to say that violent and assaultive behavior does not occur among people with schizophrenia and other psychoses. One 1990 study of 1400 families containing members with severe mental illnesses found that within the preceding year, 10.6 percent of the ill individuals had physically harmed another person, and an additional 12.2 percent had threatened harm. [23] Eight percent of offenders who murder or attempt murder have schizophrenia, and schizophrenic patients are four times more likely to be involved in violent incidents than patients without an underlying psychosis. [24] Drug and alcohol abuse and noncompliance with antipsychotic medications are the greatest risk factors in producing violent or assaultive behavior.[25] In other words, untreated schizophrenics and those who may be self-medicating with drugs or alcohol are most likely to be a danger.

This is truly unfortunate because this predilection to violence, when it occurs, is perhaps the greatest factor contributing to the stigma associated with schizophrenia and similar mental disorders. Friends and family members may understand that the violence is not the fault of the individual, but of the illness; nevertheless, a pattern of assaultive behavior cannot help but induce fear in those who are trying to care for the patient, and may make it insurmountably difficult to maintain a relationship with a loved one who has lost control. For my part, I was utterly unaware of the statistics, which was likely a blessing; my misgivings resulted from my own direct observations, which were, in themselves, incredibly frightening. It's difficult not to be frightened of someone who beats you, and who threatens to kill you, particularly when you know that they are not rational and therefore not subject to reason. I know I would have been better able to cope with my mother's violence had it had objectively observable triggers, or had it lent itself more readily to prediction. Since it was impossible ever to know what she was thinking, very rarely was I able to guess what might prompt her to threaten or strike me, and very often it was the attempt to remove myself from the range of her assaults that caused her to strike even harder. There was no winning, and ultimately, it seemed, no sense in fighting.

Few people, if any, saw this side of her behavior. While there was obviously an abundance of other witnesses to her delusions, as far as I know, I was the only victim of her ongoing violence. It is almost unfortunate that this did not occur until the height of her illness, because had it transpired during what I like to call our "psychiatric rotation," I might have found the protection I so desperately required. In the period beginning perhaps a year prior to the noticeable onset of her illness, my mother took me to several psychiatrists. The first few she eventually dropped for reasons she never specified, but the last two I was definitely seeing while she was sick. I especially recall the very last doctor, sitting hour after hour in his dark, wood-paneled office, trying to persuade him that my mother had lost her mind. For some weeks I had been reluctant to say it, because I knew I was only asking for trouble; already my mother had menaced me repeatedly with incarceration in the once-notorious Bellevue mental hospital, and I perceived her attempts at having me evaluated by these doctors as an inevitable step in the commitment process. Even then, I knew that trying to turn it around, trying to claim that my mother was the one who was mentally ill, would be perceived as teen stubbornness, the rebelliousness of adolescence, or the pathological lies of my supposedly warped and fractured mind. Eventually, however, I must have convinced him, because one day, like the others before him, he brought my mother in for a private meeting, following which, we never went back.

Had she been beating me then, had I had scratches and bruises and had lost weight because I wasn't eating, perhaps my arguments would have been more persuasive. Instead, even though I had consulted with a string of psychiatrists, doctors who specialized in mental illness, not one of them had been able to help me. But they were not alone. No one seemed to understand the severity of my mother's illness; indeed, she had isolated us so much by the height of it that, for a time, no one besides me ever caught more than a glimpse of her behavior. And even though I myself was trapped at the very heart of her illness, even though I had known her intimately for sixteen years and had watched her transformation with unspeakable horror, at first even I did not know what to think. How could I know what was real? Could my biological father really have returned after a ten-year absence? My mother claimed she had spotted him on a street corner in town. Could my sister really be waiting to drop down through the ceiling to kill us? Mom insisted she had scaled our garage with a ladder. Surely Mom wasn't making this stuff up?

I'm sure she was not. I'm sure she believed in her paranoid delusions just as fiercely as the woman Diane did. Fortunately it didn't lead her to murder. It did lead her to violence. More than that, it led her to the belief that she herself might, at any moment, become a victim. Perhaps this is why she fought so desperately to ward off those assaults that existed only in her imagination. Perhaps she sought solace in the somber certainty her suspicions gave her.

There came times in which my mother no longer felt safe at home at our little place in the suburbs, times in which we crossed the state line and stayed night after night in cheap motels, abandoning the imagined perils of our now-vacant home. My stepfather John had moved out, and in those days it was solely me and her, her and me; the only other people in our world were waiters and night-clerks, anonymous strangers that rarely spoke but merely glanced in passing at the tall, pretty woman with the surly teen-aged daughter. And as her symptoms worsened, perhaps it was only natural that she should seek to place the blame for her deterioration on her most faithful companion: the very daughter she sought to protect.

It was one of the ironies of her condition that for a long time it came down to her word against mine as to which one of us had lost her mind. How often I feared that her word would win.

POISONED

"I'M SURE YOU didn't mean anything by it," she whispered conspiratorially, clutching the wires crisscrossing her torso as if they were lifelines. "You didn't really mean to hurt me, did you?"

I didn't answer. I had no answer for her.

She raised herself; bent her back up off the angled, starched-sheeted bed, the skull-flattened pillow. "You won't get into any trouble. I promise," she assured me in her most persuasive tone, leaning towards me as if greater nearness would bring her closer to the truth.

I glanced at my mother, ragged now from our endless day of blood tests and EKGs, pitiful with probes attached to her chest and hands. Then averted my eyes and stared instead at my own hands, knuckles white on the edges of the uncomfortable folding chair on which I perched by her bedside, and wondered if they were even capable of doing her harm. Thought that if they were, that surely they would have done it already.

She bent her face close to mine, the urgency in her voice betraying the calmness of her countenance. "Just tell them what you gave me, sweetheart," she pleaded.

Her breath stunk of metal fillings and stale cigarettes, and I backed involuntarily away. Hasty and harrowed, to her my retreat conveyed confession and it prodded her on, encouraged her investigation.

"It was poison, wasn't it?" she whispered excitedly, almost hopefully, I thought. "Just tell me what kind!"

Why was she so obsessed with poison? I speculated, not yet comprehending that it was impossible to rationalize the irrational. She refused to eat at home anymore because the food might be poisoned; preferred the anonymity of restaurant fare. But then it was in my orange juice or her coffee, might have been sprinkled like salt on the eggs or buried deep in the butter, this mysterious killer toxin, by some even more mysterious killer who stalked us, who intended inexplicably to do us harm.

"It's not too late," she urged. "If you just tell them what it was, there might be an antidote. They could still save me!" She smiled at me kindly, then conscientiously ran her hands over her scalp, smoothing down the short blonde hair she'd had colored and cut in fruitless disguise.

Sometimes I even wondered if she herself was guilty of administering the poison she so terribly feared. If that was the real reason why she kept snatching my meals away at the last second, in an attack of conscience over attempting to murder her own daughter. Even I had begun to look suspiciously at my food; wondered whether I should refuse it, no matter how many meals I had lately missed. I was gradually absorbing her paranoia, cinching it to my core like the belt around my sagging jeans.

"It's not going to go well with you if something happens to me, you know," she snarled, all at once dropping her coy sweetness. "I've left evidence. They'll be able to prove it was you. You'll be locked up for good, I guarantee it."

I listened to the quiet bleeping of the machinery at her bedside and eyed the doctor staring curiously from the hall, the doctor who had been sent away after admitting they hadn't been able to find any physical cause for the searing pains in her chest, the shortness of breath. My co-conspirator, no doubt.

"And don't forget about Bellevue," she spat. "I'm your mother and I can still have you committed. Maybe it would be good for you," she concluded nastily, sneering her contempt of my supposed sanity.

It shivered through me, this worst of her threats, the familiar fear of the powerless pitted against the powerful. I imagined myself again, sealed into a strait-jacket, shrieking wildly in protest, proving my lunacy thereby. Being trundled into some dark hole and left there forever to rot, to die, while she roamed freely about, seeking, perhaps, another child, a youngster, a victim more susceptible to accepting her incomprehensible illusions.

"So are you going to tell me or not?" she snapped finally, whipping her head around as if to startle me into the truth, her hands clasping the bed's guardrails, steadfastly refusing to misbehave in public, in front of witnesses. Hanging on to the cold steel as if afraid she might forget herself again, as she had lately made a habit of doing; bruise my wrists with her claw-like fingers, or box my ears with the flats of her palms.

I bowed my head as if in contemplation, perhaps in prayer. Gazed directly into the once-familiar mud-brown eyes, hollow now, as they had become in recent weeks, vague and empty and occupied elsewhere, in vast regions of runaway imagination that I couldn't see, couldn't possibly perceive.

I meditated whether I should try to explain it to her, the irrationality of her suspicion. How could I have poisoned her? I was sixteen, and the internet hadn't been invented yet. I wouldn't have known what kind of poison would work on a person, even if I'd had access to some. And how would I have bought it, with her watching me twenty-four hours a day, even while we slept?

I stared unwaveringly into them, the eyes so unlike my own, so nearly inhuman yet not animal, either; alien eyes. And abandoned the hope of persuading them with my useless reasoning. Her world had an impenetrable logic all its own.

"I didn't give you anything, Mom," I said, turning away.

She cursed out loud. I didn't look back.

She surrendered. Accepted the doctor's discharge and took me home. But she eyed me mistrustfully as she ordered me into the king-sized bed we now shared.

"I can't force you to admit what you did," she conceded as she lay down, fully dressed, on top of the blankets. "But I still know you did it."

She clasped her hand hard to her chest and let out a gasp, as if in pain. And almost I wished I had relented and confessed to the uncommitted crime, I pitied her so.

THE DAUGHTERS

APRIL, MY POOR, sad sister April. **If only she had still been a** part of the family when I was old enough to know her pain, we might have shared something meaningful and worthwhile. Instead she's vanished between the pages of my personal history along with that handful of other scarcely known individuals who might be termed my relations.

I suspect now that she was the first to experience my mother's insanity first-hand. At the time, of course, I had no idea. I simply couldn't understand what was wrong with her, why she was always disobeying. She ran away from home repeatedly, which made Mom cry and then whip her when the police dragged her back to our apartment. She was bad, bad for running away, bad for making Mom cry, bad for making Mom whip her with that big brown leather belt with the metal buckle on it. She had to have been really bad, I knew, because Mom never hit us otherwise.

I didn't know my sister well. Technically we were half-sisters because we had different fathers, but that hardly mattered, since they were both strangers to us. She was almost eight years older than I was, and our acquaintance was like that of most children so widely separated in age – we had nothing in common. Whatever relationship we might have developed as I got older ended before it could start, as she was out on her own with a child of her own by the time I was ten. I have a handful of memories of her from my childhood. Coming home after school to find her blasting Rush or Pink Floyd on the record player in our apartment. Being subjected to her powerful and not entirely good-natured noogies. Her barging into the bathroom when I was in the tub, shouting "Little titties! Little titties!" at me years before I would even begin to grow any myself. Her years of babysitting me are, at best, foggy within my recollection; I don't think it was a job she tackled with relish or with particular care. Indeed, what I remember most about my only sibling was our near-utter lack of sisterly contact; in fact, it was an honor when we younger kids were permitted to hang out with her and her friends.

Almost everything I know about my own sister therefore comes from the lips of my mother, whose information, in light of her illness, remains highly suspect. My mother was not what you'd call a liar, but when someone is delusional, they're incapable of separating the truth from the fiction. Therefore I can't know for sure what really happened with my nephew Chris; can't know for certain if he was abused, or if April was in any way responsible for that abuse. For all I know, my mother inexplicably believed that she was and then simply took him; the story she told me later about him going to live with his father may have been untrue. After all, I never saw Chris injured or bruised, and never saw him act strangely, or any more strangely than other small children do. I wasn't around during the supposed visit from Social Services, over which I lost my room, and I never witnessed my nephew being picked up by his father, either. I'm left guessing as to the truth, wondering what was real and what wasn't, and wondering, too, what Mom might have said about me when I wasn't listening, and who might have believed it to be true.

I don't know what I lost when I lost my sister because I have very little idea of who she really was. If she truly was a crack-addicted child abuser, then I'm inclined to think I didn't lose very much. But I'm not entirely convinced that the logic supports this. For example, if she supplied her drug habit by performing as an exotic dancer, as my mother claimed, then how did that work during the two times between the ages of seventeen and twenty that she was pregnant? Or was that supposed to have happened later?

It's all very vague and uncomfortable, and the only way I could find out the truth is by asking my sister, who, even before our mother's illness, was nearly a stranger. We hadn't even seen each other in nearly two years when my mother succumbed to her psychosis, and she and my nephews were already safely away; I would not willingly have involved her in that situation, no matter what she had done.

Still, I would like to know. I'd like to know just how deep were our mother's delusions, and I'd like to know if April knew about them, too. Because when I think back on that awful period of our family life when she was repeatedly fleeing our home, I have to wonder – why, why did she keep running away? Because I know why I kept running away, and I know how it must have looked to outsiders, too, to people who didn't understand what was going on with my mother, and who must have thought I was an awful and ungrateful child for trying to leave her. Even my own stepfather – who I'm now nearly convinced never really knew about my mother's illness – dragged me back home to her after I fled one of her impromptu assaults. If no one understood what had happened to me, then maybe no one understood what had happened to my sister, either. Was it possible that Mom had had an earlier psychotic break? Had she had a previous cycle of schizophrenic relapse and remission? Perhaps April was not the perpetrator, but my mother's first victim.

But of course the questions do not end with April. What about Mom's other daughter, the one who was mentioned in her obituary? My other half-sister, Sandra Johnson, who was born between me and April. Was she good like I was, or did she run away and get beaten, too?

Wait. Who the hell is Sandra Johnson?

Did Mom really have another kid? I mean, I knew she'd had numerous husbands – at least six by my count – but another daughter? I hadn't even suspected that.

What had happened to her? Why hadn't I met her? Why wasn't she part of our family? Did her father have custody, and who was he, anyway? Had Mom given her up for adoption? Or might she have been taken away? If she was still alive, then why didn't we ever see her?

Did she even really exist in the first place?

With Mom, you never knew.

I wonder now if April knew. If she knew about Sandra and if she knew about Mom. If, at sixteen, whether she understood what it was impossible for me, at eight, to comprehend. Yet how long did it take me to understand when I was sixteen? For how many weeks did I wait and watch uncertainly before I acted, before I dared to act? For how long did I behave as obediently as a child of eight, wholly accustomed to a mother's rule?

My older sister stopped being a child long before I did.

Later on I was grateful, unbelievably grateful that when my time came, I was old enough to understand, that I had reached an age in which my own thoughts had sufficient strength and clarity to allow me to grasp what was happening to her and to us. Often I've wondered what would have become of me had I not known, had I merely accepted my mother's reality, had I followed her blindly, as a child would do. Because a child does not question a mother's truth, a child believes in the supremacy and the certainty of the parent, a child trusts in what she is told to do.

All of our parents tell us lies and half-truths, but few of these have such an impact on our worldview, few dictate how we will perceive those closest to us for the rest of our lives. I cannot know now what my sister experienced; cannot know what she suffered when she was a teen, or what she might have suffered in the eight years she spent alone at my mother's side. All I know for certain is that she, like my mother, like me, is without family. Each of us is alone, and always will be; my mother's sickness stands like an impenetrable barrier between her and me.

RUNNING AND HIDING

MY MOTHER HAS taken me to the bus station in downtown Springfield. I am confused, because we have never taken the bus, and there is nothing wrong with our car. But I am not frightened, because she hasn't yet harmed me, has only just begun to make threats. I am not worried yet about disappearing. Perhaps I should be.

The bus finally appears, its square face wobbling over the cracks and ridges in the asphalt as it approaches. I follow behind my mother as we board it in silence. Silence has become my new shield, my new armor. I can't say anything wrong if I don't speak. And when my mother speaks, I can't believe what she says and believes. I don't know why we're taking the bus, or where we are going. But I don't dare to ask her, and she doesn't tell me.

I follow my mother to two seats at the rear, and in silence, we ride. I can't look at my companion, this stranger who was once my mother, because I don't dare meet her eyes. Some instinct within me fears that she will interpret it as aggression, as an attack, like the big mean dog I pass on my way to school, who growls at me when I try to be friendly. And I don't like looking at my mother and seeing this stranger's eyes. I look at the other passengers instead. The hunchbacked old man, resting his elbow on a wooden cane. The young woman tapping her feet and consulting her watch, worrying that she'll be late. The sandy-haired man with the glasses, a baby peacefully asleep in his arms, a stroller and diaper bag crowded about his feet while he rocks in steady rhythm.

The mounting sun warms my shoulders as morning gives way to nearly noon. We are still riding, and I become vaguely aware that this is no ordinary bus like you find in the city, no commuter vehicle. It doesn't halt every few blocks like other buses, but drives steadily towards the edge of the city, stopping only occasionally to discharge its passengers. One by one they lumber down the narrow steps, blinking their eyes against the sudden sunshine before hurrying off down the street.

And still we ride. The passengers have become boring, repetitive; I, like my mother, gaze silently out the window instead. The stops become even more infrequent and the city grows sparse, dissolving into suburbs, farms, pastures; wide-open spaces where it is hard to imagine that people live.

At last, only the two of us remain, and my mother has still given no indication of how far we are going. Something within me has begun to worry, because I don't know where we are or how to get back. But surely my mother knows what she is doing?

I gaze out over the bold yellow field that runs alongside the road and perceive, just beyond the next curve, a dusty crossroads transecting our path. The bus crawls to a halt shortly before we reach it. My curiosity is aroused; we have not pulled the cord that signals a stop.

The driver has risen from his seat and is walking towards us. He is a stooped middle-aged man with a dented nose, a smattering of white hairs in his neatly trimmed beard, and a well-pressed navy-blue uniform. I barely noticed him when we were boarding; now he is the sole focus of my attention. Incomprehensible fear has begun to prickle down the back of my neck, and along my chilled spine. I don't know very much about taking the bus. But I do know that the drivers usually stay in their seats.

"Ma'am?" he says politely, addressing my mother. "Don't you want to get off here?"

"No, thank you," my mother answers. Her voice sounds timid and squeaky, a sharp contrast to the strident tones she has lately used.

"Ma'am," he repeats. "Ma'am, you have to get off here, do you understand? This is the end of the line."

"The end of the line?" she echoes, confused.

I turn to look at her for the first time, the worry and fear growing stronger. I have accepted me not knowing where we are going. But my mother is taking us there; she is supposed to know.

The driver nods, gesturing sideways with his elbow as if pointing us in the direction of the open door.

My mother hesitates. She turns to face me, and I flinch but look back, trying to read in her eyes what she will not tell me.

"I guess we'll have to get off here, then," she says. Her voice is firmer now; it carries a new trace of conviction.

She stands and clasps a hand to my arm, dragging me up after her. I stand and look at the driver, wondering what to do. I do not want to get off the bus with my crazy mother in the middle of nowhere without water or food. I do not want to be lost and left alone with her. But the driver is already retreating, already resuming his seat. He has already told us what to do.

I stumble down the formidable steps and emerge, like the other passengers, blinking blindly against the brilliant sunshine. I watch through watering eyes as the bus turns and begins retreating slowly back towards the town. My mother stands watching it, too.

"Where are we going?" I ask her for the first time.

"Did you see it?" she says quietly. "Did you hear? How he came back to tell us to get off here? This is the place; I'm sure it is."

"What place?" I repeat. My confusion is rapidly being replaced by something worse.

"He was in on it; he must have been. Otherwise why would he have told us where to get off?"

A second passes in which I can almost see it, almost believe it, and I am almost relieved. The driver did come to fetch us; he did tell us where to get off. Is my mother's theory right after all?

But in the next second, I know that it cannot be. Because if it were, then I would need to be even more frightened, even more worried about this conspiracy, this citywide plot to get us or to take us away. If my mother hasn't gone mad, then the world has.

She is surveying the landscape with probing eyes. The uncertainty has vanished from her dark visage; the lines in her face are determined and set. There is no doubt that she sees it, and that she believes it. Somehow this makes it even more frightening.

Once again, she grabs hold of my sleeve. "This way," she says assuredly, nodding towards the gleaming, windswept field.

She walks, and I walk beside her. She retains her grip on my arm, but somewhere along the way, I lose my grip on myself. I vanish, I disappear. I am lost in the field of golden wheat.

It is some hours later when I come back to myself. I know that we have been walking, but I don't know how long or how far. I am hungry and tired but it doesn't matter; all that matters is my mother, and what she might do next.

It is late afternoon or early evening when I suddenly find myself standing on a street that looks oddly familiar, and suddenly I know where we are, if not why we have come. We are in Ludlow, where my stepfather's mother lives. I have been here before.

The house looms before us, not friendly and welcoming as when Nana stands on its front porch, waving us inside, but dark and silent and lonely, its gables deepening the shadows that thicken about its entrance.

"Nana may be sleeping," my mother whispers, tightening the collar of her coat about her ears and neck. "So we have to be very, very quiet."

Why have we come here, if not to see Nana? We only visit her once or twice a year as it is, and never without my stepfather present. But we're approaching the threshold of her heavy wooden front door, and I don't dare to speak.

My mother reaches down to the worn mat which welcomes us and retrieves a key from beneath its rubbery surface. She puts a finger to her lips to warn me to keep quiet and cautiously creaks open the door, holding her own breath as if to silence its squeaky protest. And then returns the key to its poorly disguised small-town hiding place and beckons me inside.

I follow, my eyes focused on the plaid-patterned linoleum of the foyer, the flat yellow glow of my mother's handheld flashlight, the path it dimly illuminates before my tired, sneakered feet. My spirits involuntarily rise as we painstakingly descend the plush-carpeted stairs leading down to the basement. I love Nana's basement: the exquisitely carved table where she serves dinner for company and holidays, the merrily crackling fireplace beneath the stone mantle, the cozy plush armchairs tucked into its corners.

"This way," my mother murmurs, guiding me away from the comfortable heart of the room, the book-lined shelves that give it the hush of a library. She directs me instead towards the wide double-doors of the large coat closet perched in near-obscurity behind the staircase.

I wait, perplexed, while my mother very slowly, very carefully slides open one of the white-painted doors. Why is she going in there? Nana only uses this closet for storage, for coats that are too fancy for everyday wear; the regular coat closet is upstairs. Is there something in there that she needs?

"Get in," my mother says, pointing inside, casting a thin pale circle of yellowish light with her flash. I hesitate, wondering whether my hearing of the curious command is correct.

"Now," my mother prompts sternly, her long, delicate fingernails clutched upon the edge of the door, her face obscured in the thick shadows of this strange underworld.

I obey. I step reluctantly inside and find myself pushed up against a sea of cloth smelling faintly of mothballs and cedar, and I struggle with the dense pressure of the heavy coats on my neck and shoulders.

My mother forcibly shoves the cloaks aside, creating a narrow rift in the wall of wool and sturdy wooden hangers. "Sit," she orders, her voice dropping again to just above a whisper.

I sit, bunch my knees clumsily up to my chest, press them against my own thin denim jacket, and gaze querulously out at the darkened scene laid out before me: the bare table, the empty fireplace, the inaccessible armchairs.

Then my mother gets in, too, sliding the door very slowly, very quietly behind her, shutting out the dim, ill-defined outline of the fat volumes lining Nana's shelves. She joins me cross-legged on the floor, winking off the light of her lamp as she does so.

"What are we doing here?" I finally whisper.

My mother swallows uncomfortably, but there is no uncertainty in her voice when she answers. "You'll see," she says gruffly. "For now you just need to be quiet."

I hug my knees and watch through the crack between the two thin sliding portals as the light in the room dims, filtering half-heartedly in through the dusty half-windows that periodically interrupt the walls near the ceiling. I listen to the brisk footfalls and clanging noises overhead that must mean that Nana is home or awake now, and making dinner. I am exhausted, but I am not weary; something tells me that I must not sleep.

Suddenly I hear, then feel, heavy footsteps descending the stairs.

"Dad!" I nearly cry, half-lurching up from my seat as he comes into view. My mother grabs me and pulls me back down, forcing her hand over my mouth.

I wrest my face away from her hand, but I fall silent. I haven't seen my stepfather in quite a while, ever since he disappeared from our house some weeks before. Perhaps he has been staying with Nana?

My stepgrandmother is setting the table; she and my stepfather are having dinner. They are talking to each other, but not about me, or about my mother; not once do they mention why he is here. I watch them through the crack in the doors, once again wondering what I should do. Part of me wants to leap out of the closet, to let them know we are here, but the desire to be good, to obey, still holds me too greatly, while the desire not to be caught hiding and spying grows greater still. Even in the moment, I am keenly aware that this evening may be the turning point in this whole affair, that the key to my mother's behavior may lie in what's transpiring on the other side of these closed closet doors. And I want to know.

But nothing happens. The minutes turn into an hour, and still I am paralyzed, unable to decide whether to act or hold back.

"How long do we have to stay here?" I grumble at last.

"As long as it takes," my mother murmurs in response.

"But what are we waiting for? Why can't we...?"

My mother's clammy hand once again clasps itself firmly over my mouth. I turn towards her; see the narrow ray of light emanating from the dining room chandelier reflected in the whites of her eyes. How fiercely it pierces and illuminates her dark pupils, giving them both hollowness and fire.

"Someone is after us," she informs me. "Someone very bad. Someone... who wants to hurt us. Do you understand?"

I shake my head, and she releases me. "Who would want to hurt us?" I ask.

My mother directs her gaze back out towards the room, where my stepfather and his mother are clearing the table, their footsteps tramping heavily back up the stairs.

"That's what I'm trying to find out," my mother replies.

I peer out once again at the empty room and surrender; stop trying to understand it. I shift position, unbend my knees and cross my legs. I lean back against the long woolen coat that hugs and softens the hard wall behind me; watch as my mother does the same. I settle quietly beside her, bold and alert, silent and stiff, prepared to wait the prolonged, bitter hours until the running and hiding are over.

DETACHMENT AND DISSOCIATION

THERE WERE INCIDENTS in life with my mother, particularly early on in her illness, that were so unreal that I cannot even picture myself living through them as I was then, a young woman; immature, perhaps, but full-grown, nearly ready to be out on her own. Certain of these moments were so baffling, and so bizarre, that in my mind they could only have occurred far, far off in some distant, perhaps even pre-sentient past. And not to me as I knew me; they had to have happened to someone else. A child, perhaps, a curious observer of her mother's behavior. Not the teen-aged Lori, but a younger, more innocent child. Gloria, who feels what I could not feel, who fears what I could not afford to fear. Cannot afford to fear.

Her stories are fiction. Wouldn't they have to be?

When I originally wrote the preceding segment, that's how I wrote it. "Bus Ride" and "Hide and Seek," which are reproduced in the Appendix, tell Gloria's fictionalized story of running and hiding. In some ways, her account is more real to me than my own. It's certainly more believable.

For me, this bewildering day was a turning point in my mother's illness. It was simultaneously the day I became thoroughly convinced that she was insane, and also the last day I had even a smidgen of doubt. There were many worse days that followed, many that were more dangerous to me personally, many that were more frightening. But those days, as awful as they were, were never unreal. By the time we had reached "A Safe Place," I had internally adjusted to my mother's warped sense of the truth; I had accepted that it had little relation to everyone else's understanding of the world and of the people in it. I was therefore able to recognize those events as something that had occurred in my own world, and within my own plane, even if the limits of my reality's boundaries had been severely stretched.

But the day of the bus ride, the day we spent in my stepgrandmother's closet – those never felt real. They didn't feel real when I was experiencing them, and they don't feel real to me now. It's as if I can see them happening from a distance, as if I can see my mother, and how she behaved, but I am merely watching; I am not really there.

The fictional Gloria is present in these stories in a way that I could never be. The little girl is able to experience feelings that should have been entirely foreign to the sixteen-year-old me. She is unable to doubt her own mother, even when her mother is clearly wrong. She follows direction, and obeys without thinking. She experiences the natural confusion of a small child when confronted with circumstances that are grotesque and perplexing, yet she cannot question their essence, their reality. Her world and her mother's are one, simply because her mother says they must be.

I had spent my whole life obeying my mother. She had the power, and the authority, and she had kept it because she had never abused it. These were not feelings that I could, very abruptly, no longer have at sixteen – not after only the first few weeks of my mother's illness. Yet I was forced to behave like a six-year-old girl; forced to treat my new world as if were entirely real, and only beyond my comprehension. I was helpless, and powerless, and unable to act, incapable of defending myself against the monster hiding in the closet because I did not yet know what it was. To this day, this conflict creates such consternation in me that Gloria's story makes more sense to me than my own. This happened to her, not to me.

I think now that what I may have been experiencing was the beginnings of what is called dissociation. This is a natural psychological phenomenon in which the mind intentionally distances itself from events that are too emotionally painful to process.[26] It's generally considered to be helpful, and even adaptive, because a mind that is focused on its own pain or terror is less able to manage stressful situations or physical trauma. The vast majority of dissociative disorders occur in children who have experienced ongoing abuse or repetitive trauma, and in extreme cases, these may lead to the well-known phenomenon of split personality, not to be confused with schizophrenia, which is an entirely different disorder.[27]

My experience did not go that far. But whatever was happening inside my mind, whatever it was my brain did to help me to cope with my situation, there is no doubt that the bulk of my emotions were shut down for several years following my mother's illness. I don't think I cried more than once the whole time she was sick; there was no energy to spare on such fruitless emotions. I was rarely sad or even angry; rather I was resigned, and grimly. It was useful to me, being that way. I could not have lived for eighteen months in a state of unending horror, and for many more months as one of the homeless and hungry; the panic and misery would have undone me. But I had no moments of unreasoning terror. I had no moments of uncontrollable panic. Even in those instances when I wondered whether my life was ending, I was fully capable of relying on reason, of making plans and of making decisions. I was able to act in ways that would preserve me, and I don't think that would have been possible had the paralysis of fear taken hold.

I've often seen the same phenomenon in other memoirs written by people who have endured traumatic events. They can be describing the most awful experiences, yet there's so much detachment, so little emotion. They, like me, might remember what happened to them, but they don't feel it; they can't let themselves feel it. This is how they've survived.

I both lost and recovered myself during this incident. The line between my mother's reality and mine was firmly established, and never again did I question where it should be drawn. And the painfully raw feelings that I experienced, the bewilderment and the crushing fear, this is when I began to tuck them away, to lock them up in a box inside my mind and only release them nearly twenty years later, when my mother died.

Whatever remained of her, the little girl in me, was sent away on a bus going nowhere and vanished in a field with no name. She was confined to the darkness of a closet and never emerged into light. In my mind, those are the places where she yet lingers.

THE FEAR

IN 1991, ABOUT a year and a half after I ran away from home, I received the first letter from my mother. She had hired a private detective to track me down, she said. I had an address at the University by then, so I assumed it couldn't have been that hard. Much later I learned that she'd actually weaseled the information out of her favorite, my old friend Josh. How he discovered I'd run off to California I guess I'll never know, because that was a closely kept secret; even some of my dearest friends couldn't have said where I'd gone. I had kept it quiet from my teachers as well, even those who had written me recommendations; no one besides my guidance counselor knew I'd applied to school out of state.

I'd had a terrible year. I'd left home with fifteen hundred dollars, a beat-up old station wagon, and the expectation that I'd be attending college in the fall. But several months later I was still living in my car on the streets of Berkeley, shivering sleepless through the chilly nights by the Bay and walking around picking up bottles and cans all day trying – and often failing – to get together enough money for food. I hadn't been able to rent an apartment because I was underage. Without a place to live, it's nearly impossible to get a job. I got to the point where I was eating so rarely – sometimes only once every two or three weeks – that I couldn't keep food down when I did eat.

I didn't know then that I was starving. I didn't know then that I would spend much of the next two years living in my car and not eating. What I did know was that those prospects didn't terrify me nearly as much as the thought of being hauled back to my mother.

This is still better, I'd thought night after night, kneading my rumbling stomach with my fingers while unattainable visions of pizza and hamburgers swam around in my head.

It was better.

How petrified I was when I received that letter, at the mere sight of that handwriting on the envelope, those big swirling loops with which she formed all of her letters. I would have recognized them anywhere.

"You're over eighteen now," I reminded myself, shaking as I turned the frightening paper rectangle over and over in my fist. "Legally, she can't force you to come home."

Unfortunately, people who are mentally unbalanced aren't always concerned with legality. Maybe she could no longer call the police to come and get me, like she did my sister, but she had other options. She could hire another detective to do it, or worse, she could come herself. I had been re-accepted to college and was living in the dorms by the time I received that letter. Would the Resident Advisor in charge of our floor object to letting a girl's self-professed mother into her room? Who knew to what lengths she might be willing to go?

That fear, it never quite went away. And when my mother wrote to me the second time, a decade and a half later, I was almost more afraid than I had been the first time. I'd just begun dating a man who had two young children. I had nightmare visions of her appearing on his doorstep with a butcher knife or worse. I sent out warnings to everyone I knew. Judy Green-Hair is back. Watch your step. Because you never know; you just can't ever predict what someone with an untreated psychotic illness might decide to do.

By then I'd been on my own for sixteen years. I'd moved back and forth across the country twice and had had more than a dozen different addresses. But I still didn't feel safe. I was thirty-three years old. But like my mother, I had yet to find a safe place.

A SAFE PLACE

"IS THIS A safe place?" she inquired softly, her contrived timidity carrying the persuasive force of conviction. Her delicate hands, with their long, well-manicured nails, twitched where she held them behind her back.

The middle-aged man in the doorway didn't know how to respond. How could he? His eyes took a stab at me, crouched behind my mother's tall figure, made even taller by the puffy blonde wig she was wearing now as a disguise against her very dangerous but very imaginary enemies. I shot him back a look that revealed nothing. I'm sorry I can't help you, sir.

"I don't – I don't think I can help you, ma'am," he answered at last, perhaps taking my mental cue after all. He glanced back towards my mother, not quite meeting her eye.

"All right... Thank you, sir," she replied politely as she turned to go. The man retreated inside, closing the door quietly behind him, as if afraid that a loud noise might summon us back. But she had already grabbed me by the wrist and was dragging me down the sidewalk. I marveled at how firmly those seemingly frail hands could clutch bone, how the nails pinched and imprinted my skin, always enough to hurt, never enough to break or bleed. I reminded myself that I ought to be grateful that I wasn't broken or bleeding.

The next house was broader, loftier, an elegant two-story Colonial with wood-shuttered windows and dusty pink rosebushes set in a tree-lined yard. When my mother rang the bell, a little girl of about eight answered the door with as much alacrity as if she had been hiding behind it.

"Is this a safe place?" my mother asked again. The child stared at her, stared open-mouthed at the funny-looking wig, at the tight jeans and sneakers and tie-dyed T-shirt that were supposed to allow a middle-aged woman to pass for a teenager, someone her daughter's age. I fixed my own gaze on the little girl, mentally commanding her to go back inside. She failed to obey.

A young woman appeared behind her and laid her hands upon the child's shoulders. "May I help you?" she inquired kindly, after sizing up the unusual pair on her doorstep and erroneously deeming us harmless.

"Is this a safe place?"

The woman frowned and peered around my mother's shoulder towards the wide, empty street. "Is something wrong?" she asked. "Did your car break down? Are you – hurt?"

My mother sighed and bent her mouth towards my ear. "I don't think this is it," she whispered with evident disappointment. "We appreciate your time," she said aloud to the woman, who stood, like her daughter, gaping open-mouthed as we made our way back down the concrete walkway towards the street, the familiar sinewy handcuff again controlling my arm.

We had to wait some minutes at the next house, a one-story ranch with an ancient sedan in its driveway that wore the dust of decades of disuse. As the music of the doorbell faded away, it left in its wake the cadence of a soft shuffling, a shuffling that grew gradually more audible as the slippered feet that generated it drew near. At last she appeared in the doorway, a suspicious-looking elderly woman who peered out at us through thick-rimmed glasses and the slotted screen of her outer door, which she did not open. The town was funny that way. Small enough to get you to answer the door for strangers, but not enough to make you feel quite comfortable doing it.

"Is this a safe place?" my mother inquired again. "I heard that there was a safe place around here." Perhaps somewhere inside that impenetrable mind she'd decided that some further explanation was in order if we weren't to be stuck wandering door-to-door around the neighborhood all night.

The old lady hemmed and hawed, noisily rearranging her dentures while she attempted to formulate an answer. I pitied her. It was a hard question. And then, as if struck by a sudden inspiration, she burst out loudly, "Have you tried the church?"

Again my mother turned to me, and her eyes were lit up like

Roman candles as she shouted gleefully, "That's it!!" She pushed me down the walkway before her as if she had finally decided that this was more efficient than dragging me along behind her. But I didn't like it, not being able to see what she was doing. I tripped on a crack in the sidewalk and stumbled, causing her to stumble slightly over me in turn. Back unbroken, she nonetheless cursed loudly as she resumed her place by my side, clutching at my shoulder and elbow awkwardly before again fixing her grasp on the trusty bones of my wrist.

But recalling her purpose, so nearly attained, she rapidly recovered her good cheer. "We look just like sisters, don't we?" she said brightly, clearly pleased with the undeniable success of both her mission and her disguise. I didn't answer.

It was a long walk to the church. The whole town was out, it seemed, enjoying the cooler evening air that was temporarily supplanting the hot humidity of an early New England summer. I rigidly ignored the curious stares and unspoken inquiries, concentrating instead on my mother's claw-like grip on my arm, the power of the outer pain and not the pain inside. I was so focused that I failed to notice a friend of mine approaching from the other direction until he had nearly passed us. He slowed, with deliberate nonchalance, and, nodding almost imperceptibly, met my eye, his expression telling me plainly that he didn't know what to do, either. I hadn't been in school regularly for some time, and the exact state of things was no longer known to anyone but my mother and me.

I didn't think I could communicate it with my eyes. "Help me," I mouthed silently, and he flinched, but caught himself and continued walking. I thought it was an intelligent decision, not to reveal himself to her until he had executed his plan, whatever it was. By the time I dared to look back, he had vanished into the thickening dusk. Some minutes passed but he did not return, and when no one else came swooping in to rescue me either, I stopped looking. I wasn't sore. What had I expected him to do? What could he have done?

It was a Catholic church. I had only ever been to the Church on the Green. This one was grander, but gloomier, or maybe that was only the effect of the darkness that had by then entirely blanketed the houses and lawns of the town. There was no one else inside it, neither priest nor parishioner. My mother's muttering echoed and reverberated throughout the chill vastness of the high-ceilinged chamber, a chamber empty of people, of God, of salvation.

"You sleep in there," she ordered, pointing to the cramped confessional that was to be my bed for the night. "I'll be in the other one."

I crawled inside the narrow box, sat down with my knees curled up to my chin, sat silently and listened for a break in the silence and waited. I did not pray. I waited until the church bells chimed the hour and then waited until I thought it must be almost time for them to chime again and still it was silent. And then I jumped up and ran.

We collided at the exit, those powerful hands with the long, well-manicured nails at once finding a firm grip on my wrists, both of them this time, slamming me hard against the heavy double doors so that my breath caught in my chest.

"This is a safe place!" she snarled through gritted teeth, barely raising her voice, knowing that shouting was unwarranted and unnecessary. "And you're not going anywhere!"

She was right. Safe or not, I wasn't going anywhere.

The "safe place" episode deeply, deeply disturbed me. If I'd had any remaining doubts as to the horrifying extent of my mother's sanity, that evening removed them. I learned two things that night, and they changed me forever. One, that even my mother's incredibly public displays of lunatic behavior were never going to result in official intervention, even when she had a minor in tow. No one would ever, ever be there to help me. And two, I could never know if I could escape her. Until this point, I had thought I could get away if I really had to – simply run off into the ether if that's what it took to save my own life. I thought I had options. Now I was no longer sure.

This acknowledgment of the precarious hold I had on my own existence would, in one night, transform my perception not only of my mother, but of the world around me. I have never been antipathetic towards authority figures, but I've never had much faith in them, either. The system didn't fail me – it barely knew I existed.

THANK YOU
AN OPEN LETTER TO THOSE WHO STOOD
BY ME DURING MOM'S MENTAL ILLNESS

I'VE INTENTIONALLY REFRAINED in this memoir from going into detail regarding my own social relationships except where they directly intersected with incidents involving my mother. Thanks to the mixed blessing of social media, I'm still in occasional contact with a number of those I knew then, and have even crossed paths with some of them from time to time at weddings, etc. I have no wish to discomfit anyone with stories they might deem too personal to be publicly shared, and the simple fact is, while the tale of how two friends and I drove up to Canada to smuggle booze when I was a senior might be entertaining, it really has no place in this memoir.

That being said, I have never stopped being deeply, deeply moved by the level of friendship shown to me by those with whom I was close. It suddenly became much more difficult, being my friend. My mother wasn't merely unbalanced and delusional – she was scary and dangerous. On top of that, I had the new and rather unpleasant reputation of being the daughter of the insane Judy Green-Hair. I doubt whether there was a single kid in our school of twelve hundred who didn't know who I was, and I didn't like it. To this day I remain strongly averse to being the center of public attention.

During the great period of isolation, my mother essentially withdrew me from all society. At some point even her favorite, my friend Josh, was no longer welcome, and since the rest of my friends, including my boyfriend Jesse, were allegedly Satanists, there was no question that they had to be firmly excluded from our private lives.

That changed when I was a senior. While much of our crowd

had graduated the previous year, I was welcomed back into the fold of most of those who remained. And while I can't say I properly appreciated this at the time, I realize now how impossibly hard it would have been for me had I had nothing and no one when I went back to school. I would have been a total pariah. At least this way I was a pariah with several noteworthy exceptions.

This is not to say that I did not encounter difficulties, even among my close friends. One long-time friend later told me that she breathed a sigh of relief when I turned thirty, because if I was still asymptomatic by then, it meant I was unlikely to get my mother's disease. Another pot-smoking friend told me I shouldn't smoke because it might drive me crazy, just like my mother had been. These types of incidents eventually led to a constant sense of being evaluated, of being watched in ways that kids who were "normal," kids who were not perceived to be at risk for going mad, were not. If other teenagers misbehaved, they were rebelling. But if I misbehaved, I was clearly insane!

I have included in the Appendix a guest blog post that I wrote for stigmafighters.com, a site dedicated to telling true stories of mental illness. "You Don't Have to Be Mentally Ill to Suffer from the Stigma Associated with Mental Illness" details my frustration with experiences like these, and my resentment over being judged by my mom's mental illness. In my heart I know that I was probably being overly sensitive, and that I probably overreacted to what I perceived as ill-treatment. After all, children of schizophrenics do inherit a genetic predisposition for the condition; the risk of a child developing the disease when one parent has it is thirteen percent.[28] My friends and acquaintances were not necessarily wrong in exhibiting caution, but to me their concern seemed unwarranted and premature. It was like the equivalent of telling a healthy teenager that she could not eat a slice of cake because her middle-aged mother was diabetic!

But by and large I am grateful for the way I was treated by the kids I knew well, and who knew me; many grown adults would not have been so forgiving. And my friends were not the only ones who were able to separate me from my mother. My teachers, in general, did not treat me differently, even though every one of them must have known what had happened. There were others, too, who learned to look past Judy Green-Hair and see that I was my own

71

person; I remember one male acquaintance in particular whose bright smiles at me never altered, whose attitude towards me never visibly changed. As a consequence, I developed a terrible crush on him after Jesse had gone off to college, and although nothing ever came of it, I never forgot that boy's kindness. Little things, maybe, but they made my life livable. And for me, livable was a worthy goal.

The support I received meant more to me than most people could ever imagine; it forced the snide remarks and crude insults of the bitchy and ignorant firmly onto the high school dump heap, where they belonged. The kids who turned up their noses at me with such perfect disdain, the people who shrieked or edged away when I walked by, they've all been forgiven because their identities have all been forgotten, every last one. They don't matter to me because they don't exist anymore, not on this plane or on any other. But the friends who kept me, the friends who helped me, they could not be forgotten; they will exist for me always, even when they are gone.

Dear Friends from My Youth,

June of 2015 will mark the twenty-fifth year since our graduation – the twenty-fifth anniversary of the day I left home.

Some of you I have not seen in those twenty-five years. Some, I fear, I won't see again. I've never been one for reunions or for keeping in touch, yet you might be surprised at how often I think of you still. Lately my memories of you have drawn even nearer to the forefront of my mind, as I think back on the day that I ran away – and as I think back on all the other days when I wished that I had.

In the spring of last year, I learned that my mother had died, six years before, in 2007. In the months that have passed since, I've written a book: *On Hearing of My Mother's Death Six Years After It Happened: A Daughter's Memoir of Mental Illness.*

I know that to you I don't need to explain; that I don't need to tell you why I say mental illness, and that you'll understand why it took so long for me to hear of her death. And perhaps you'll understand, too, why I think of you now more than I have in two decades; why I'm writing this letter years after you should have received it.

We were all of us helpless during Mom's mental illness,

adolescents with limited resources and limited experience. There was little we could do to manage my personal situation, and nothing we could do to manage my mother's psychosis. Yet each of you did something, some small thing, perhaps, to ease my distress and lessen my pain. Each of you, in your own way, helped me move on, helped me escape, helped me survive.

So to you, Michelle, my long-time chum, I want to say thank you. For letting me call you at midnight when I got too lonely to stand it; for letting me talk and also letting me listen. For persuading your parents to permit me to use your phone number on my college applications, so that Mom didn't have to know everywhere I'd applied. Maybe it didn't seem like much to have done to help out a friend. But it got me my scholarship, and that salvaged my life.

To you, Karina, let me also say thank you. For helping me plan and then helping me move; for corralling our dog back into the house while I was frantically packing, for knowing that even in that desperate hour I wouldn't have wanted him to get hurt or get hit. For being my friend in spite of what anyone thought; for never giving a damn what anyone thought. For that, Karina, I thank you.

George, my former friend, my later lover, how can I thank you? You did so little, and yet so very much. You came when I called. You've always come when I called. I think you still would.

Josh, my old friend Josh. What a wonderful time we had while Mom was insane! For so long you were my sole solace, my sole support, my sole source of happiness. I'll never understand why Mom, even in the depths of her dementia, took such a shine to you and your charms; why her suspicions never turned upon you as they did the rest of our friends. You were the only person, kid or adult, that she would still allow into our home, and what a dreary, depressing place it must have been for a cheerful and energetic young man to enter time and again. Yet you did. Week after week and day after day, you came and kept me company, kept me alive, kept me sane. You perhaps can't imagine how much I looked forward to your visits, or how often I've wondered what impelled you to make them. Or how hard it hit me when they finally came to an end, when even your most good-natured arrows could no longer pierce my mother's thick armor. Yet the light of your smile, that you shone upon me and that you even shone upon her, lightened my burden and smoothed my transition. Those afternoons that we spent side by side were the most precious gift I had ever received. I thank you for giving them to me. I will never forget them.

Jesse, sweet Jesse. Quiet and shy, lacking, like me, even a license, you weren't well-prepared to swoop in like a knight and come to my rescue. No, you weren't able to take me away – but you never went away, either. You continued to love when there was no reason to love; you continued to wait when the waiting seemed without end. You were there when I emerged, blinking hard against the sun now burning my eyes, and you were there when I sank again into black pits of despair. There were times when I couldn't have counted the days since I last saw you – and there were more when I didn't want to count those that would pass before we met again. But I knew that however many had passed, and however many more would, you would still be waiting, and that was everything to me. Thank you, Jesse. Thank you for being with me.

And thank you, friends, for listening and for reading my letter. I know that we may never again meet, and may never again speak. I know that you'll understand why I haven't written you sooner, and why I won't ever write you again. And I know, too, that you'll forgive me for so long maintaining my silence. Because what's a mere twenty-five years between friends?

Forever yours,
Lori

MOMENTS

I GO TO the window and peek out. My stepfather is standing on the sidewalk, his usually placid visage purple with rage. Someone has told on me.

"Get down here!" he shouts.

I am surprised to see him. I have always liked him; he has always been kind to me. But he rarely takes a strong role in parenting – that's Mom's job. Besides, I thought he had moved out. Could this mean…?

"NOW!" he roars.

It is the evening after my detention. I have gone to the house of a friend who lives near the high school. I have made no plans beyond surviving the night. I have no need of making them now.

I slip on my jacket and tiptoe down the stairs. My friend and her family are standing at the bottom. I glance at my friend. I don't look at her parents. I already know she's going to be in trouble for hiding me.

In the car on the way back to the house, my stepfather yells at me. It is the only time in eight years that he has ever yelled at me.

"Do you know how worried your mother is?' he snarls. "Don't you dare pull anything like this again!"

I look out the window at the pretty, quiet streets of our suburban town. The yards are empty. The sidewalks are empty. I am empty.

There is no one to help me. Why won't anyone help me?

It is prom night. I have been waiting for weeks to see if my mother will decide to let me go. I am stunned that she is even considering it.

75

I think it must be some kind of cruel joke, pretending she might. I can't remember the last time she let me leave the house by myself.

But she does. I don't believe it even as I'm slipping into my shiny green dress, even as I'm tucking the five-dollar-bill she's given me into my bra because I don't have a purse. I don't even believe it as we're driving away, or sitting at dinner, or arriving at the hall, no mother in sight. It's my big night out.

My boyfriend looks adorable. Jesse always does. I'm surprised that he's still my boyfriend. Who dates a girl like me? But he's as sweet to me as ever. It's the main thing I will remember about the dance in years to come. The way he looks when he sees me. Someone still cares.

I have to be home early. My friends make sure I get there on time. We don't talk about what might happen if I don't. We don't talk about anything.

I'll never understand why she does it. Why, for one night, she lets me pretend to be normal. But I will always be grateful to my mother for that. For letting me live a little. Before I forget how.

I am sitting in the back of my station wagon, holding a letter from Jesse. I rented a post office box before I ran out of money, so at least I can receive letters. And I have a book of stamps, so I can write them. There isn't much else to do at night after the library closes. I have taken to lingering in the Young Adult section because none of the other homeless people hang out there. This is what I tell myself. But in fact, I'm re-reading all of the books I read when I was in junior high – the ones I remember, anyway. I can't get enough of other teenagers' problems.

I am hungry. I am always hungry. It doesn't hurt very much anymore but I still can't stop thinking about it. Sometimes the letters help me forget for a while. Sometimes they don't.

It's cold in the station wagon. California is supposed to be warm; I never dreamed that it would be so cold at night, even in summer. I have had a car accident and my rear side window is broken. I have covered the hole with a sheet of plastic and some duct tape, but it's still breezy in there. One night I wake up to find a man in a mask peeling off the tape.

"Hey!" I yell, not too loudly. I want him to go away, but I don't want anyone in the neighborhood calling the cops.

I'm holding the letter up under my dome light, reading and re-reading it. It's a very long letter. But Jesse is a long way away. Just like everyone else is.

I don't know that running the dome light will drain my battery, and in the morning it's dead. My hair is slimy and my clothes are stinky and I'm embarrassed to ask someone for a jump start, but I do. I have to. I have to move the car to a new neighborhood so the people in this one won't ask the police to come and remove me. I'm learning. After a few months I'll be an expert. And I'll finally be eighteen.

It's lonelier after that. I don't dare to run the dome light at night anymore. No more letters to keep me company.

It isn't as painful as you might think. I've already been alone forever, it seems. I've long since given up expecting anyone to come along and help me. No one will.

We are sitting in a coffee shop in East Longmeadow, my mother and I, at two stools along the horseshoe-shaped counter. Her with a cup of black coffee, me with a cup of hot chocolate. We have been going to another restaurant in town for breakfast but I suppose something there has spooked her because today we've gone to this other place and she still hasn't gotten me anything to eat. I don't complain. I have hot chocolate.

There are truck drivers here, or, at least, men who are talking about trucks and driving. They're chatting cheerfully with one another and I wonder if maybe Mom feels at home here because she spent years waitressing at a truck stop. I don't mind the men, but I do mind the horseshoe-shaped counter because it means they keep looking at me, and looking at Mom, and looking back at me. I can't even guess how we look. I long ago stopped wanting to know.

Some of the men leave and the place grows quiet. I hear music playing. The oldies station. I like oldies. Mom takes a refill on her coffee. I sip my hot chocolate and listen.

I recognize the song that's playing. It's one of my favorites. I almost smile.

"Build Me Up, Buttercup." It's a special song, mine and my friend George's. He often plays it for me in his car and we always sing along when he does. Loudly. We're both very loud when it comes to singing.

I'm listening to the music and thinking of George and the last time I rode somewhere with him and suddenly I feel something welling up within me, something I have not felt threatening me since this ordeal began.

Tears.

They're out before I can even launch an effort to stop them. They cascade over my eyelashes and down my cheeks in a rush, and I panic. Hostages learn quickly to betray no emotion. You don't want to draw attention to yourself when your kidnappers are near you.

The men who remain are still looking at me and I'm terrified that they'll see me cry. Will they say something to me? To my mother? What will happen then?

I have no escape from their eyes. I'm not even allowed to go to a public restroom by myself.

I lift my cup up in front of my face and force down a big sip of my now lukewarm drink. It presses painfully against the lump in my throat. My mother is gazing vacantly out the window and I grab a napkin and dab very delicately at my eyes, hoping she won't notice. But the tears keep coming. I fight to stop it but I can't; that damned song is still playing and I think if I hear the line about breaking my heart one more time I'll dissolve into a puddle and have to be washed away like the drips of coffee my mother's cup has left in a ring on the counter.

The song ends. It's been the longest two minutes of my life. But it's over now. I stop crying. Tears are a luxury I cannot afford.

But that song will always make me cry, every time I hear it from then on, even ten, twenty years later, it will still make me cry. How could something that once brought me such pleasure now bring only pain?

I don't turn it off, though. I always listen straight through to the end. No matter how badly it makes me feel. Or how hard it makes me cry.

A five-dollar bill. Fluttering there on the sidewalk, yet miraculously motionless in the early-morning breeze; flapping just enough to attract my attention without flying away.

My feet clamp down upon it, hard. I squat down fast and dig it out with greedy fingers, then crush it into a ball and stuff it deep in my pocket.

It's barely past dawn. I finally have money, and nothing is open. I wonder who dropped it, who was benign or foolish enough to toss away five whole dollars as if it were nothing, as if it meant nothing. Ah, well, he or she would be thinking in self-consolation. It's only five dollars. It's not life or death.

I glance at the barricaded door. The curtains haven't been drawn yet, but the too-familiar sign still stands in the window. Breakfast, two dollars. Coffee, eggs and toast. I almost smile. I sit down on the sidewalk, waiting. It smells of stale vomit, but it isn't mine. I was down the road a ways when my last meal came up on me.

There's a click and the door opens behind me. I jump up and run inside without speaking. I lay the bill conspicuously on the counter so they will know that I have the money. They're very kind. They bring me extra coffee and packets of jelly that I eat plain when I run out of toast.

It lasts longer this time, and it stays down longer, too. But I'm sorry because it comes up right next to the library where I like to spend my rainy days. Still, it's something, isn't it? Finding five dollars. Not a matter of life or death, maybe. Not just yet.

It is in one of the in-between times, when Mom has decided to let me out for a while. Perhaps she has grown fearful of Social Services. Perhaps she intends to inspect the house from roots to rafters and wants me out of the way. Perhaps she's simply sick of watching me all day and all night. I don't know. I know better than to question it.

My friends and I are at a hotel for a school function of some sort. I don't remember exactly why. Band, or perhaps Key Club? It doesn't matter. I have reached a point where nothing seems very real.

I am wearing an orange dress my mother bought me. It's hideous, but I don't realize that until later. Jesse is with me. He is holding me. I am grateful for that.

We are on one of the upper floors. We are beside a railing. It overlooks the center of the hotel. We are talking. I don't know what about.

I can see us standing there together. Me in that ugly orange dress with my hair cut short, my face buried in his shoulder. Him with his arms wrapped in a circle around me. I can see it, see it as if I'm above it and not inside it, and in my mind I've gotten up onto the railing and I'm teetering there, on the verge of going over, and I don't know how to stop it; don't know if I even care anymore about trying to stop it.

"Lori," Jesse whispers, clutching me tighter. "Lori, I think you're going insane."

How does he know?

They echo in my brain, these words he's spoken, and for a split second I see myself swaying there on the edge of the rail, my mind and body preparing to topple into the welcoming infinity that awaits me.

Then I'm back in the hallway in Jesse's arms, watching as she goes over. Crazy me, down over that railing, plummeting several stories to the floor far, far below.

I catch a glimpse of her face as she falls. For a second she stares back at me. I hardly recognize her. She hardly seems to recognize me.

I look away. I don't see her land. But I know she's gone. I'll never see her again. Somehow, I know it.

Did I ever tell Jesse how thankful I was to him for that? For pulling me back from the edge of insanity? I don't think I did.

Something tells me he already knows.

It's the middle of October. I am eighteen years old. I celebrate my birthday by breathing a sigh of relief. I'm no longer a runaway.

I have gone for a walk. It's after midnight, but I can't sleep. Walking is all there is to do.

I see an empty can in the gutter. I'm surprised. Berkeley has many homeless people who collect bottles and cans. Some of them are well organized. They push shopping carts with trash bags knotted all around them. They keep the streets very clean.

I pick up the can. It's dirty, but so am I. I carry it as I walk.

I keep walking. I see another can, then a glass bottle. I pick those up, too. The idea forms that maybe this doesn't have to be an idle stroll. I begin hunting in earnest, my eyes fixed to the ground. I need a bag.

In a ditch by the side of the road, I finally find one. Not a grocery bag; a black garbage bag. Half-filled with bottles and cans! My heart beats faster. There is real money here.

I've crossed the line into the next town, and I'm still picking up bottles and cans. The bag has grown heavy. I have been walking for hours. I decide it's time to go back. But now I don't know where I am.

I turn, and turn again. Nothing looks familiar. I'm finally tired. I could sleep for hours and hours. I'm longing for the comfort of my station wagon, of my pillow and sleeping bag. Please let me get home.

Finally I see a freeway. I climb the on-ramp. I don't know what else to do. It's the only way I know to find my way back.

It's just beginning to grow light. I trudge along, the bag slung over my shoulder like I'm the poor man's Santa Claus. I don't stick my thumb out. When I hear a car pulling up behind me, I pretend not to notice.

Then I hear a short burst of police siren. I drop my sack and turn around. Do I put my hands up?

A uniformed policeman climbs out of the cruiser and strides towards me.

"May I see your identification, please, Miss?"

I fish my wallet from my pants pocket and give him my license. He takes it back to his cruiser and vanishes inside for several minutes. My heart thumps in my chest. Is he checking up on me? What will he find?

Rush hour is beginning. The traffic is growing louder. The wind of the cars and trucks going by blows past me so hard I'm struggling to keep my feet.

The policeman returns. He gives me back my license.

"Why were you walking on the freeway, Miss?"

"I got lost."

"Lost how?"

"Going for a walk."

"Where do you live?"

"Berkeley." I wonder if I hesitate before I say it.

He hesitates before answering. "Are you carrying any weapons?" he asks me.

Strange question, I think. "No," I answer. "Only my Swiss army knife."

"May I see it?"

I dig it out of my jacket pocket and show it to him. He examines it curiously.

"You're not carrying any other weapons?" he says again.

I shake my head. Again I wonder why he's asking.

He casually reaches out and pats my jacket pockets, inside and out. It's my Massachusetts winter jacket. The inside pockets are big and bulky enough to hold miniature machine guns. But there's nothing to find.

"You can't walk on the freeway," he admonishes. "It's dangerous."

"I didn't know how else to get home."

"I'll give you a ride," he suggests. It's almost a question.

I don't know what to say. He mustn't know where I live. I don't know what the law does to people like me. I know I can't stand to be locked up again.

"Come on," he urges, handing me back my knife. "I'll give you a ride."

I glance at my big garbage bag, still crumpled on the ground at my feet.

"We can take that," he says quickly. "Look, I'll put it right here in my trunk."

I watch as he does it. He ties up the top, being careful not to spill any of the contents. Then he opens the passenger side door.

"Usually we don't let people ride in the front," he explains. "But in your case I guess I can make an exception."

It's a good half-hour drive. He doesn't ask me any questions. Instead he talks, about his family, about being a policeman. He uses his loudspeaker to order another driver to slow down. I'm suitably impressed.

When we get to Berkeley, I direct him where to go. We arrive at the narrow side street where I'm parked. I still don't want him to see my car.

"I can get out here," I say. "It's just a block down."

He's surprised. "I can take you."

"It's a dead end. Pain to turn around in," I improvise.

He doesn't insist. He pulls over and lets me out of the car. I walk back to the trunk. He opens it and gives me my bag.

I sling it back over my shoulder. The weight of it feels satisfying again.

"Sure you'll be all right from here?"

"Yes, thank you, Officer." My voice cracks as I say it. This is the most I've spoken in weeks.

I look down the street. I spot the station wagon, maroon against the white of the fence just beyond it. Home.

I take a dozen steps towards it. Then I turn around.

"Thanks for the ride!" I yell.

The policeman waves. I wave back. I don't smile. But I almost feel like I could.

Mom and I are spending the night at a motel. One of many. Mom goes into the bathroom, leaving her purse behind. It's hanging open, and I see something familiar inside it, something that was stolen from me. My bank book, the old-fashioned kind where the teller records your deposits and withdrawals line by line and then tallies your new total. A small blue folder that may hold the ultimate key to my liberty.

I have no money without it. Without money, I have nothing. I have not been allowed to get a license, and I do not know how to drive. Perhaps I could run away on a bus. If only I had the money to purchase a ticket.

I am sixteen, but I have never taken anything from my mother's purse. Strange how dirty it feels. Stranger still, when I realize I have nowhere to hide my purloined loot.

I unpack my nightshirt from Mom's suitcase and fold the book into it. She emerges from the bathroom and I go inside to change. I tuck the book into the front of my underwear. I hope she won't notice it there.

I walk out of the bathroom with my nightshirt stretched down to my thighs. She's sitting on the bed, staring in that vacant way she has now. I smile uncertainly at her. She lunges.

The force of her body slamming into mine takes my breath away. She forces me down onto the bed. I somehow manage to get my legs bent and my knees up against her chest, so that she's balanced above me in some creepy caricature of a mother and child at play.

"You give me that bank book!" she shrieks. "Give it to me!"

I don't answer. Instead I reach down to check that it's still where I left it.

She hits me, hard, on the ear. It hurts like hell, but still I don't say anything.

"Give me that bank book!" she screams, hitting my other ear. I can't believe how painful it is. I force my knees up higher but her arms are too long; I can't get away from her reach.

She hits my ears again, each of them in turn, again and again. Somewhere in the recesses of my brain I finally understand what the term "boxing someone's ears" means. I know now why it's such a bad thing to do. I cup my hands along the sides of my head like shields. It doesn't help much. But I take it. I'm determined, now. I'm not giving up that bank book.

There's a loud banging on the door. She rolls off of me to go and answer it. I sit up and press my back against the wall and try to catch my breath. I wonder what they've heard. I don't think I've made a sound.

She says something to the man at the door. He answers, too quietly for me to hear. Not police, then. Briefly I consider whether I should go to him anyway and ask for help. I decide not to bother. I already know how that song goes. It will be worse for me if I try.

I get up to finish getting ready for bed. She sits down on the mattress, glaring.

I've never struck her. I haven't even fought back against her. I'm simply not capable of beating up my own mother.

And now I see that I don't have to. Because maybe I can't stop her from hitting me. But she still can't make me surrender that bank book.

I have no vision of victory, no thrill of triumph. But somehow knowing that I've still got that bank book in my underpants inspires me with resolve.

It is only much later that I realize this. At the time my mind shifts direction of its own accord, without any conscious intervention on my part. But somewhere inside me a switch flips and I at last seize hold of the conviction that this situation is not going to resolve on its own.

I think of sitting in my step-grandmother's closet, my knees pressed to my chest, coats bundled up around my shoulders while I watch my stepfather and his mother through that narrow crack in the door. Watching and waiting. Not knowing what to do. Not daring to do anything. I think of the long bus ride that we take to get there, and the longer walk through the countryside of rural New England that follows it. How many times does the bus stop along the way? How many opportunities for me to make an escape? But I take none of them. Not because I am weak, or foolish, or afraid. Because I don't know yet that we have already reached the end of the line, my mother and me.

I know it now. The time for watching and waiting is over. Reacting to my circumstances is no longer enough. If I want to survive, I have to take action; I have to take control. I must have a plan. I've already taken the first step. My first step towards freedom.

ESCAPE

THERE ARE EXACTLY thirty days left in the school year when I attempt my first real escape.

I've formulated a plan. It's simple enough, when you break it down mathematically, which I have. I have a thousand dollars in the bank. I have my precious bank book. I sleep with it under my pillow. Even Mom doesn't sleep as lightly as I do now.

I know from recent experience that I can rent a room in a motel over the state line in Enfield – just six miles from my school – for thirty dollars a night. I also know from recent experience that I can get by with hardly eating at all. And I know how long Mom spends in the shower – long enough for me to stuff some things in a backpack and then run down the block and across the street and into the woods lining the border. I don't know what I'm going to do when school is over. I cannot yet plan that far ahead. I have not even considered whether it will be tiring, spending four hours a day walking back and forth to my school. Surely I must be capable of anything.

But of course I'm not. It's a pathetic scene, and it replays itself several times that day:

A teen-aged girl, a lime-green bandanna tied around her hair and chin like a babushka, steps up to present herself to a middle-aged motel clerk.

"I'd like to rent a room," she announces, poorly feigning nonchalance.

He looks her up and down, his eyes filling with disbelief, perhaps even a bit of concern. "Um, I'm sorry, Miss, but you have to be twenty-five to rent a room here."

She adjusts the bandanna uncomfortably. Evidently it's not the brilliant disguise her mother always seemed to think that it was.

So much for my plan. I walk, clutching at my backpack and my bandanna. If I were still capable of feeling, I'd be terribly depressed. School is almost over for the day. It's miles back into town. And once I get there I still have nowhere to go.

I consider my options. I don't seem to have any.

I see the mall just ahead. I need water and a bathroom. And my mother will be looking for me. I can't stay out on the street where I might be seen.

I trudge up to the big double doors and duck inside. It smells like new clothes and old arcade games and freshly baked cookies. It's a good smell.

I find a pay phone. There aren't many people I can call. Some of my friends' parents don't want their children to have anything to do with any situation involving my mother. Some of them don't want their children to have anything to do with me. In case I go crazy, too.

I call Jesse. It's long distance, and costs me a lot of quarters. I listen through a dozen rings. There's no answer at his house. I hang up and my quarters come clinking back down the chute. I use them to call George. He answers. Jesse is with him. Something has gone my way.

"Can you come get me?" I say. My mouth feels numb as I say it.

"Where are you?" George asks.

"At the Enfield Mall."

He doesn't ask why. Twenty minutes later, they've arrived. The part of me that still recalls the feeling of happiness is grateful.

They are two of my closest friends. They are no longer allowed at my house. My mother insists that they – like me and several others of my friends – are Satan worshippers. She's seen all of our names on a list down at the police station. I wonder what she was doing at the police station. I wonder how a town the size of Longmeadow could possibly have enough Satanists to warrant maintaining a list. I wonder how she even knows my friends' last names.

"What are you doing here?" they ask me at last.

"I ran away from home," I answer.

I don't tell them the rest. I can't.

They don't ask. I'm glad. We wander around for a while. Eat ice cream sundaes. I like ice cream sundaes. And I have money in my pocket now. But it can't buy me what I really want.

It gets late. George drives us back to town. He brings me home with him. His family puts me up for the night. It's a pleasant break from Mom. But it makes no difference. I can't stay there forever. In the morning I still have nowhere to go. It's only a matter of time before she finds me again.

My plan has failed. I have failed. Once again, I'm lost. I don't know what to do.

It makes for a good story, though. Years later people will still be laughing about it.

"Hey, Lori, remember that time you ran away to the mall?"

Ha ha, I laugh along, embarrassed. Funny, funny joke.

I never tell them the whole story. But the next time, I make a better plan.

ALONE

MY MOTHER WAS an Italian, and she was a Catholic, both of which are known for having large families, yet by the time of her illness, she had hardly any relations remaining. Her mother and father both passed away in their early fifties; only one grandparent survived them, and he had retired to Florida some decades before. We never saw her older brother and his wife after they moved to New Hampshire, and an ongoing family feud seems to have permanently severed the oft-troubled relationship between my mother and her younger sister. Evidently the last straw was when she wore a white pantsuit and no underwear to my mother's wedding, after which she was no longer welcome at our home or at family functions. An assortment of cousins disappeared with my childhood, and if there were other distant relations, I never knew they existed. A whole series of in-laws had come and then gone; even my father's family did not deign to keep track of their own blood relation. Even my sister, my mother's own daughter, had removed herself from our family and the family home; the circumstances surrounding my mother's illness ensured that she and her children would never be a part of our lives again.

That was it. All accounted for, and every one of them absent. That was my mother's extended family, and now it is mine.

We were both frightfully alone in the world, my mother and I. Yet, before her sickness, I never perceived it. Yes, our family functions had always been rather small. Dinner at Easter and Thanksgiving and Christmas could be served at the kitchen table; once my sister was gone, my mother and stepfather and I often went to a nice restaurant instead. There was no pile of cards waiting for me on my birthday with checks for five or ten dollars inside them, few cards at Christmas to line our windowsills or fireplace mantel. There were no reunions, no weddings, no funerals; no baby showers to attend for our future relations, no graduations for the young girls and boys who had grown into young women and men. Yet I never missed them, these people who existed for others, but not for me. We didn't need them, because we had each other.

That was how I always perceived my mother. She was the only person in my life whom I thought of as permanent, as fixed, the only person I conceived of as my family forever.

The men my mom dated and married – I had learned from a very young age not to take them too seriously. Wise children know that new dads never lose the status of boyfriends, that they only remain fathers for as long as they remain lovers.

My mother and I parted ways when I was too young to comprehend – or even care about, really – the nuances of grown-up relationships. I had always accepted the men in her life as just that – the men in her life, who might also, temporarily, become a part of mine. They were not permanent, and they were not my parents. Not even John, who was my stepfather for all of eight years, and who made a kind and determined effort to be my father. In fact, he was the only one of the series of men in my mother's life who truly tried to build a relationship with me, and he did so successfully; he really was a good man. But then why did he walk away when my mother got sick? Why did he leave her in the throes of psychosis? Why did he abandon the stepdaughter he had tried so hard to win over to the clutches of a delusional and unbalanced woman? Why did the only adult in our lives who might have helped me, helped her, helped us, leave me to manage my mother all on my own?

For many years, I assumed that John and my mother had split up because of her sickness – that she had tossed him out in one of her rages, or that he had found her sudden violence and unpredictability too tough to handle. I thought that perhaps he didn't understand that she was mentally ill, that, as with my teachers and friends, it would take time and exposure for that fact to sink in, time and exposure that he didn't get. It wasn't until I began writing this memoir that another possibility came to my mind, and it had to do with another one of my mother's letters.

Some ten or eleven months after my mother's condition developed, while she was immobilized from her later foot operations,

I discovered a letter she had written to a man whose name I recognized, one of the regular customers at her old restaurant. Always hungry for information regarding what was transpiring inside her fevered mind, I labored through deciphering her missive only to learn something that I did not need to know – that my mother had been having an affair with him.

I can't say I thought much of this information at the time – in fact, as soon as I figured out what the letter was about, I stopped reading it. My mother's sexual escapades held no interest or insights for me, and it's difficult to hold someone responsible for sins they commit while they're insane. In fact, since the letter was undated, I couldn't even be sure that this had transpired before my mother and stepfather split up; it just seemed unlikely that it would have happened at the height of her illness, or after her operations. But what if it wasn't a part of her illness at all – what if it had preceded it? It wasn't until almost thirty years later that I began to wonder if this affair had more significance than I had initially granted.

In "Moving In, Moving Out, Moving On," I describe the first known incident of my mother's illness – the first to involve me, anyway – in which she tried and failed to gain custody of my sister's first son. The weeks following that episode are a blur of confusion to me. I remember that my stepfather was away on a business trip when it started, and I also remember thinking that he'd be able to help her when he returned. Except that by the time he got back, we were already gone, off on our tour of motels across the state line, my mother in her silly disguises, towing her truculent daughter behind her. And when we finally did return to the house, he had moved out – not that my mother ever told me he had; I simply had to figure it out from the fact that he never came back. I never saw him again after that, except for the one night when he came to fetch me from my friend's house after I'd fled. How odd that had seemed to me at the time. Why was he the one chasing me down if they had split up?

But now a more sordid explanation occurs to my mind. What if my stepfather was never actually away on a trip? All along I've assumed that the initial round of motel stays was prompted by my mother's absurd fear of my sister spying on us from the attic, of my biological father lurking about town, waiting for his chance to kill us. But what if these were delusions she subconsciously invented as a means of avoiding the truth — that she had to vacate the house to

91

give my stepfather a chance to move out? Did he learn about the affair – perhaps even find the same letter that I did – and order her out of the house? Was she afraid of him? Was this the reason for the disguises, for hiding out in the closet in his mother's house, where he'd gone to stay? Was either the affair or his discovery of it in fact the precipitating event that sent her over the edge?

I can't ever know, and I won't ever ask. Deliberately opening someone else's old wounds to sate my own curiosity is not a cruelty of which I am capable. However, I did see my stepfather once more, when I was in my early twenties. One summer I took a trip back to Longmeadow to visit Jesse, and, driving by the old house, saw that my stepfather's name was still on the mailbox. I guessed that he must have moved back in after my mother moved out. On a whim, I stopped in to say hello and was very glad to find that he had a new wife and two new babies. He was still only in his mid-thirties, and I thought it was nice for him that he had this chance to start again. I recall wondering at the time how he had explained the stuff about my mom to his new lady. It can't be easy to tell someone that your last wife had gone crazy.

But maybe that's the wrong question. Maybe he didn't tell her, because maybe he didn't know. Maybe he wasn't aware that my mother was coming with me to school to protect me. Maybe he hadn't heard the paranoid stories about my father and sister. Maybe he hadn't seen any of her disguises, or maybe he assumed that changing her look and cutting her hair were merely a womanish whim. And if he did personally witness her strange behavior, perhaps he merely chalked it up to the strain of their separation. Perhaps this is why he was so angry with me for running away, because he literally had no idea that I was in danger. Perhaps she had called him, crying, begged him to go and find me, if he had ever cared about her, if he had ever cared about me.

I was certainly correct in thinking that "Dad" was only my acting father, because when his relationship with my mother ended, his relationship with me abruptly ended as well. Yet this presumption on my part may have been my gravest error. Because I never questioned his absence, and I never fought for his help. I was too prepared to assume that I had been abandoned, too ready to write off John as simply the latest in the line of men in my mother's life. I don't think I was entirely to blame for this presumption. That night he screamed at me for running away from my mother after she had attacked me – it dashed any hopes for his support that I might have had. But who knows what untruths she may have told him? Because somehow I doubt he would have left us to suffer had he truly understood our situation. I find it hard to imagine that this man who had spent eight years in our lives could simply walk away without caring if my mother ended up in an asylum, or if I ended up dead at her hands. But whether he knew it or not, the end result was the same. We were abandoned, and he did walk away. I had no one else to turn to for help, because my mother and I had no one else.

It's one of the hidden dangers of isolation, and it hurt my mother as much as it did me. My mother had such a seemingly full social life when she was working that it's easy to forget that she had very few friends. For a long time she had been close with our neighbor Nancy, but she died of breast cancer when I was maybe eleven. I can't recall her ever hanging out with her girlfriends, or attending social occasions; I can't recall her and my stepfather going out with other couples, or throwing a party except for their wedding. Did my mother have any friends?

Maybe she didn't. Maybe, like many of us, she was friendly with folks that she worked with but somehow never forged any deeper connections. Maybe moving from house to house and town to town like we did prevented her from forming any lasting bonds with the neighbors, or from hanging on to the few friendships she had. Maybe leaving behind the poverty that had plagued her for most of her life had its unexpected downside, because in the suburbs the moms don't sit out on the porch on summer evenings, gossiping with the other mothers; they sit inside with the air conditioning on and order in because it's too hot to be cooking. Maybe when your children are grown and you're not in school, either, it's harder to meet people your own age or with whom you have something in common. Maybe Mom would have fared better in the apartment, where she had people who knew her, neighbors who saw her from day to day; maybe she would, at least, not have had to battle her condition all on her own.

Was she lonely? I would guess now that she was. When she was forced to quit working because of her back and her feet, she couldn't have had much to do every day, which may have made her ever more painfully aware of her aloneness. With only one teen to look after, and housework and dinner preparation only taking up so much of her time, her days may have dragged, seeming endless. And while I don't believe that this triggered her illness, of this I am certain – it did prevent her from getting treatment.

Because no one noticed. No one noticed how sick she was. Once my stepfather was gone, there was no one left who could notice. Had I not still been in school, she wouldn't even have had reason to clash with the school board. Indeed, had she gotten sick in mid-summer instead of early spring, no one might have realized that I had gone missing at all. It's horrible and it's haunting, and it isn't just her.

We live in a society in which such social isolation is perfectly possible. And in the current era, it's become even easier for people to be alone. We work from home, we do our shopping online, and for those of us who haven't lived in one place our whole lives, those of us without family friends or kids we knew from school, forging close relationships can be daunting at best.

If my mother had had one close friend – just one close friend who might have recognized the true nature of her sudden decline – she might have been saved. A friend would have realized that she had changed, or at least would have noticed that she'd stopped making contact. A friend would have been worried, would have urged my mother to seek help, to get treatment. An adult friend would have had the ability to do what an adolescent could not – convince the authorities that something had gone terribly, terribly wrong with a woman she had once known very well.

In the world of mental illness, schizophrenia is notoriously tough to treat, even for those patients who can afford the best care. There are numerous medications that can be effective, but the character of the illness itself often prevents sufferers from realizing that they are sick.[29] The delusional nature of the disorder can make schizophrenics suspicious and wary of medications, can give them fears of being poisoned with the drugs designed to help them, and can make them distrustful of the doctors and nurses assigned to their care. Plus schizophrenics are least likely of all to seek treatment, because often they do not believe they are ill; thus, they are most in need of friends and family members to persuade them to accept medical intervention.

And although I personally don't think loneliness was a decisive factor in what my mother became, the unfortunate fact is that folks who are mentally unstable are more likely to be lacking those social connections, especially those who are seriously ill. The very nature of certain mental disorders may make it more difficult for sufferers to relate to other people, to form those circles of social support which so frequently prove helpful in other illnesses. And while schizophrenics do not usually commit violence against others, if you examine stories of mass shootings, for example, you will often find that the gunmen have two things in common: that they are loners, and that they are believed to be mentally ill.

This may not be a problem that we, as a society, know how to solve. Perhaps social isolation is an inherent effect of severe mental illness as well as a cause. But its potential consequences are not open to doubt. My experiences and those of countless others clearly illustrate what may result when mental illness goes undiagnosed and untreated. And while it's easy to have sympathy for the victims, let's not forget that the sick suffer as well. I nearly lost everything because of my mother's illness, but so did she. Both of us ended up in the same place – without love, and without family.

THE UNIVERSITY

THE SCHOOL YEAR has ended. In the last two weeks, I was allowed back. I don't know why. All I know is that at last, I have completed my junior year. And in spite of everything, with honors.

The summer drags along. I have not yet figured out what to do about Mom. As it turns out, I don't have to.

"You need to get your license," she growls at me one day through tightly clenched teeth.

I'm stunned. The lack of license is what's keeping me here.

I don't ask why. I know better than that. She tells me anyway.

"Your stepfather and I are getting a divorce."

It's not a surprise. Recently I have discovered a letter my mother had written several months before – to her lover. Seems she was having an affair. All along I've thought my stepfather moved out because she's insane. Now I wonder – does he even know?

"There will be some money from the house, but eventually I'm going to have to go back to work," she continues. "I need operations on my feet so I can wait tables again."

"What kind of operations?" I ask. I know she has foot problems, but I haven't realized that they're this bad.

"Big ones," she grunts. "One foot at a time. I'll be on crutches for months, maybe a year. I won't be able to walk or drive."

A skylight opens up in my mind, bathing it in rays of brilliant sunshine. A car – a license – Mom on crutches – freedom!

She teaches me to drive while her feet are still functional. It's uncomfortable being in the tiny Chevette with her. I'm always afraid she'll grab the wheel and run us off the road. Even the sound of her breathing scares me. It's worse when she tells me she's made plans for us to move.

"Where to?"

"Florida. After you graduate. So you should plan on applying to colleges there."

My mind races. I cannot let her take me to Florida. No, no, no. I might disappear and no one would ever even find out I was missing.

"And I want you to get another part-time job," she continues. "We'll need the money."

My head spins as my heart begins to sing once more. A job, a job again! More money for my fund – more money for my freedom! I will simply have to escape before the journey to Florida. I must.

Mom has her first operation and spends her days sitting in her rocking chair. Not rocking, just sitting. Never before have I seen such pain in a person's face, a twisted mask of it that takes weeks to subside following each surgery. It's almost more wretched than the face of her dementia. Every so often I fetch her pain pills, dropping them gently on the end-table beside her, still not daring, even with her disabled, to come too close. They don't seem to do much. She often has tears in her eyes – silent, agonized ones that fill me with pity. Some part of me is glad that I have not left her to suffer through this alone.

School starts again. I'm a different person than I was the year before. Notorious in a very unpleasant way. How I long for the days when I was only a nerd.

Fortunately I don't have much time to think about the other students. I'm frantically busy. I apply to ten different colleges and show my mother eight of the applications. To the universities in California I give the address of the P.O. Box I've rented at the post office in town. I pay the application fees myself by purchasing money orders with my waitressing cash. And I arrange with a friend's parents to let me use their phone number for my West Coast interviews.

I have my own room again. My mother doesn't want me accidentally kicking her sore foot in my sleep. It hardly matters. I sleep more often at my desk than in my bed. I bust my butt on homework and in between studying and assignments I apply for thirty-five different scholarships. So many applications, so many essays – it's almost more than my schoolwork. It's worth it. I'm awarded eight of them, including a half-tuition scholarship from the Florida university my mother thinks I'm planning to attend. She's pleased with my industriousness. She can't imagine how much more it means to me than it does to her. I will need every dollar.

The real coup comes when I get the news from U.C. Berkeley, a fat envelope shoved carelessly into my post office box like last season's Christmas card. Four full years, paid tuition plus room and board. Every poor student's seemingly impossible dream – the free ride! And best of all, Mom doesn't even know I've applied there.

My mother's immobility has created an uneasy peace between us. Mom seems to realize that she shouldn't push me too far, particularly now that she's entirely dependent on me to run her errands and shop for her food. I attend school and go to work and am even allowed to see my friends again. I avoid her eyes and stand across the room from her to say goodnight when I come home. She yells at me from the other side.

My current world still stinks. I dread the day when my mother's feet will recover and feel terrible for thinking such things. She seems almost unaware of our recent past. To me it is still very much a part of our unpleasant present. Yet I can't help but feel optimistic when I look to the future. That, at least, seems to be coming together in my favor.

I don't know, of course, that it will all fall apart once I leave home the following summer. I'm unaware that the dollar amount of my Regents' scholarship will be based on my previously calculated financial need – and that because of my stepfather's prior year's income, I will only qualify for an annual honorarium of five hundred dollars. So much for college. Once again, so much for my plan.

But I haven't come this far to give up now. The U.C. system offers application fee waivers for students in need. I reapply to Berkeley, using the free typewriter in the local library to complete the forms. I'll get in, but will I win the same scholarship again? It's too late for me to go anywhere else – how would I even pay for the applications?

And I've got more immediate problems. I have been assuming that I only had a few months of killing time on the streets of Berkeley before school began. Now suddenly I've got a potential lifetime.

I have no money left, zero dollars and zero cents. I've already been through every crack in the cushions of my station wagon and dug out every lint-covered nickel. I have no money for food, let alone for rent. How am I supposed to find work?

It's late autumn. I have been living in my car for nearly five months now. The gas gauge has been stuck on "E" for weeks. I don't even change neighborhoods at night anymore – I just move down a few houses.

I grow desperate. And in my desperation, I grow conniving.

I see a "Wanted" sign in the window of a local bakery as I'm standing outside it, drooling over the pastries on display. I clean up as best I can and apply for the cashier's job. I give the address of the last shared apartment where I was denied a room. I tell the manager I have just moved in and do not have a phone. The next day I go back to follow up. To my immense surprise, they have decided to hire me. I think they must be desperate, too.

It's a minimum-wage job. I make four-something an hour. I will need at least three hundred a month for rent, if I ever find a place. But I get to snack on the day-old food. I am delighted to survive on lunches of crusty white bread and stale sugar cookies.

It's another month or so before I find a place to live. I try to cover up the sleeping quarters in the back of my car, but some of the other salespeople at the bakery are still suspicious. Funny how they are too busy gossiping to feel in the least bit sorry for me. Finally one of the other cashiers has a room available in her four-bedroom apartment. She is stunned to learn that I have been living in my car all this time. Seems she believed my story about the place at the other end of town with the three older men and no telephone.

Then more good news. I am reaccepted to Berkeley. I file paperwork with the financial aid office, a very clinical letter describing what happened with my mother. I'm not yet able to talk about her in any other fashion. But it serves the purpose. I am awarded another Regents' scholarship and recognition as an emancipated minor for financial aid purposes. When I attend the awards luncheon, I am stunned to discover that some members of the staff recall my application.

"Oh, you're Lori Schafer!" a woman I've never met says. "You remember her, Bob? She's the one who wrote that essay!"

"Oh, right, that one about freedom! Say, it was too bad you weren't able to come last year..."

I'm blown away. Seems I will be attending college after all.

The sailing is far from smooth. In my second year of school there will be massive bureaucratic issues in the university system that will prevent me from receiving my living allowance until almost the second semester. Once again I'm forced out onto the street and to surviving on one peanut butter sandwich a day.

Yet it's not as bad this time. It's that difference again, between having little hope and none at all. Plus I've bought a van, an old '69 Dodge, against just such a contingency. It is much more comfortable to live in than the station wagon, and when I'm driving around town the three other '69 Dodge Van owners who live in Berkeley honk and wave at me. Besides, it reminds me of Scooby-Doo's Mystery Machine, and that makes me happy. Once I even have company, a fellow student from my cultural anthropology class. We've been assigned to write papers on one another, and I'm actually pretty proud of the candles I study by, the blackout curtains I've made so that no one can see inside, and the cardboard-box nightstand next to my sleeping bag. In his paper he describes me as a case of downward mobility, but I have trouble accepting his conclusions. Surely this is a step up?

Winter comes, and still no financial aid. The van, while more spacious, is nearly as drafty as the station wagon and I start to have trouble staying awake in class because it's too cold to sleep at night. I've had to reduce to half a sandwich a day and I'm growing desperate again.

I'm way ahead of where I was, though. I can shower at the university gym, even rinse out my clothes there. People stare, but I'm so long past caring about looking foolish or pathetic that it barely registers. I apply for a job as a desk clerk in a large rooming house, using my old trick of a fake address and no phone. Once again I'm amazed when they take me. Better yet, they have a vacancy. It's the smallest room I've ever seen – maybe twice the size of the van – but I haven't got much to put in it. It's two days before Christmas. I can't remember ever being so happy at Christmas. For the first time, I have my very own place indoors, with no roommates or anything. Freedom!

Two weeks later, the building manager quits on short notice and recommends me for his job. I am completely unqualified for it, but the owner does not seem to mind. I nearly fall over when he makes me the offer. Twelve hundred dollars a month – plus a full apartment! It's all I can do not to hug or possibly vomit on him. It's a full-time job, but the hours are flexible and I don't think twice about taking it, school or no school. I have never even dreamed of having so much money. And the apartment! Bedroom, living room, full kitchen, and bath. Everything I own fits in one of the closets.

I've barely even gotten used to living indoors and here I am, moving again, into an even bigger and better place. I find myself sitting on the floor of this apartment, gaping in awe at the wall-to-wall carpeting, at the tall ceilings and solid walls surrounding me, at the radiator steaming cheerfully in the corner, at the cushy mattress I've inherited from a tenant who was moving out and left it behind. There are blinds on the windows but I have drawn them so I can see the moon shining down on the street below. Winter nights are beautiful when you're not stuck being out in them.

And that's when it comes over me that I've made it. It's over. I've finally made it.

My joy is indescribable. It is, I suppose, the kind of joy that only people who have known despair, true despair, can ever comprehend.

It is only years later, when I've finished college and the strain of my ridiculous schedule has ended, that I have time to think again. One night I'm going through my files, deciding what I want to get rid of before I move. I'm thinking about the first time I moved, about how nervous I was, driving around waiting for my mother to leave, for her to hobble on her slowly recovering feet to the restaurant across the street for dinner, as she had taken to doing. I'm remembering how frantic I was during that frenzied hour of packing, how much time I had spent preparing for it, how long it had taken me to choose only those bits and pieces of my old life that I absolutely could not or would not leave behind. It is a habit that will last a lifetime. Never again will I be able to move without conducting this purge of my belongings.

In a manila envelope marked "Personal," I find it: my mother's letter. I read it again, laboring over the oddly formed curves of her vowels, the strange large loops of her consonants. It's a nonsensical letter, filled with scraps of news I care nothing about and questions I would refuse ever to answer. It expresses no love and no remorse; it refuses to acknowledge my intense pain and offers no comprehension of what I have suffered. It's a stupid, stupid letter.

It disgusts me. It disgusts me so much that I go over to the sink and burn it, then wash the ashes down the drain until there's no trace left of it.

And that's when it finally hits me that it isn't over. It isn't really over, after all.

It can never be over between her and me.

ONLY A DREAM

EVERY SO OFTEN, I have a dream about my mother.

The dreams differ in story, but never in setting – they take place in a little ranch-style house in the suburbs, very much like the one in which I was raised. The characters, too, are always the same. My mother and me, living peacefully together in our family home.

Even in the dreams, I always find myself puzzled by the arrangement. It's been twenty-four years since I lived in the same house with my mother, and when the dreams begin, I find myself wandering cautiously about, like a time traveler who has been plunked down in the midst of an unknown scenario and who is uncertain of what she will find.

Mom is never insane in the dreams. At least, she does not seem to be. She has no delusions, makes no murderous threats or wild accusations; is indistinguishable, in fact, from any other run-of-the-mill mom. Oftentimes it develops that we are still part of a family, she and I, a rather ordinary mother and daughter with a rather ordinary mother-daughter relationship. I might be in the kitchen cooking while she's taking a shower, she might be coming into my room to wake me for work; there might even be a man in the picture, yet one more father to add to the list.

No, there's nothing extraordinary about Mom in the dreams, nothing to suggest that she's unwell or unbalanced or in any way a danger to herself or to me. Yet somehow I know, somehow I always suspect that it's a cover, a well-formed mask or disguise. Somewhere inside I sense that something's not right. Somewhere inside I know it, I feel it. I can't fall for the lie.

I begin to plan my escape. Even in my dreams, I plan my escape; I determine how quickly I can go and be gone, what I need to take with me, what I won't leave behind. I can acquire new clothes, a new job, a new home. A new life.

But I never make it. I never get out of that house before my apprehension wakes me, before I snap to alertness as suddenly as if I hadn't been sleeping, wondering in that instant when she's coming to get me, wondering how I could have been so stupid as to allow myself to be drawn back into the trap. How could I still be living with her?

And then I remember. My mother is dead now. Gone. Passed on. There's no need for me to keep trying to leave her, no reason for me any longer to fear her.

Because surely this is what the dreams are about? My lasting anxiety, my residual fear?

Perhaps. But sometimes I wonder whether it's not the end of the dream, but the beginning part that reveals what I'm reluctant to consciously feel. Whether that image of home and the two of us in it is the real dream that I was denied, the real reason I sometimes revisit that place that should have been mine, that place that should have been ours. A home. A family. A mom.

Yes, sometimes I wonder. Then I remind myself that it's only a dream.

FAREWELL

I FOUND MY mother's obituary long after I'd stopped looking for it. I'd searched, numerous times before, seeking news of her, of how she was doing. It was difficult, though, never knowing which one of her many married names she might be using, or where exactly she was living. Maybe if had looked more closely or more often, I would have found out fewer than six years after she died.

It was unnatural, the way things ended between Mom and me. You're supposed to grow out of being a teenage girl and learn to relate to your mother as a real person, not just the woman who tells you what you can wear and when your curfew is and to get your homework done. At some point you're supposed to get to know her.

When she sent me that newspaper clipping about her restaurant, it made me wonder if perhaps she was better, if perhaps she had gotten the treatment she needed. For a moment I was even proud of her, pleased with her success. That was the Mom I remembered, the single mom who had kicked my drunken father out for pushing her down the stairs and who had continued waiting tables to support us long after her feet failed her. I myself had been built on her model. The example she had set was what made it possible for me to stand living on the street and starving; she was the one who had taught me how to survive, and eventually even succeed.

But that Mom didn't exist anymore. I couldn't have had a normal relationship with her because no amount of loving tenderness on her part could have persuaded me of her sincerity. Because unfortunately, that's how it is with psychosis. In some ways it's no different from cancer or lupus or any one of a hundred dreadful diseases; the person suffering from the condition didn't ask for it and can't control it. Except you don't lose trust in someone who has cancer. You're not afraid of someone with lupus. But you can't ever guess when a psychotic person might lash out in unexpected, even violent ways. Or when you might be on the receiving end of it.

Two times and fifteen years apart my mother went to the trouble of hunting me down so that she could send me letters. But neither time did she ever express remorse for what I had had to endure as a result of her illness, nor did she ever apologize for hurting me or hitting me or making me the laughingstock of adolescent small-town suburbia. Not once did she even hint at being sorry that I'd been made homeless and hungry because I'd had to run away from her lunacy and had no one but myself to rely on for money or support and never, ever would.

That told me everything I needed to know about her mental state. She had not recovered. Perhaps she never would.

I guess that was my last chance. To accept the hand that had been extended.

I'm not sorry I didn't.

I don't blame my mother for what happened to her. Even back then, I knew, I understood that this had nothing to do with her personally. She was sick and she needed help, help she didn't get. Help I couldn't give her. If I felt alone and helpless, how must she have felt?

But the truth is, I haven't missed her much, not the way she was when I left her. You can't get too nostalgic over a person when your last recollections of him or her are rife with a fear that overrides any affection you once felt, that obliterates all of the good memories that preceded the many months of your own personal pre-death purgatory. I don't love her and I don't hate her. In fact, I don't feel much of anything at all for her anymore. The woman I left behind was a stranger to me. And except in the general sense of wishing them well, you don't have feelings for strangers.

Yet, when I read that obituary…

I did feel something.

It wasn't much. A catch in my throat. A heaviness in my chest. A handful of tears that threatened to fall, then sank back behind my eyes like raindrops on a mud-drenched field in spring.

But it wasn't for her. It was for me.

Because I do still feel sorry for her sometimes. For that innocent sixteen-year-old girl who used to be me. For the life she might have led. Had she had circumstances that allowed her to live it.

I said goodbye to that girl a long, long time ago. The very moment I said my last goodbye to my mother.

Yes, I bade them both farewell. But I never mourned either of them. I merely let them go.

Maybe it's time, now that Mom is gone for good. Maybe it's time to cry over the wonderful woman who raised me and cared for me and who was stolen away by some mysterious illness from the people who loved her. Maybe it's time to pity her the loss of all of her daughters, to feel sad that she died without even one child by her side, because she didn't deserve that. Few mothers do.

But maybe it's time, too, to speak the final words over the death-place of that young woman, whose life was shattered so many long years ago, years that still resound like yesterday to the grown woman who will never forget them. She, too, can never come back.

They can never be reconciled now, not the mother and the young daughter who left her, nor the mother and the older daughter who might have liked to have known her. The last chance of bringing them together has gone, swept away by seven sentences in a newspaper obituary. The last I've heard, and ever will hear, of the woman I still call Mom.

That girl, though; she still has one last chance to speak. To be heard. To be mourned.

To be let go.

CRANBURY, NEW JERSEY

EXCITEMENT AND TERROR. These are the words that describe my last weeks at home, the last weeks preceding my graduation.

The tension has been steadily building, both between me and my mother, and between my inner and my outer self. I don't know if my mother senses it because her grip on reality is still open to doubt. She has stopped making those crazy, delusional claims and has focused her paranoia on my behavior, accusing me of drinking, of skipping classes, of having sex, of late-night sneaking out of the house. She's right about all of it. I have spent my life behaving, obeying, being the good kid, and the good daughter. Where has it gotten me? I'm done with it now.

Does she know she is losing me? I often wonder. Sometimes I perceive that she's holding back, that she is intentionally refraining in her accusations because she knows her grip on me is tenuous and ever-relaxing. Perhaps she did not realize when she allowed me to get my driver's license that she couldn't hold me; perhaps she was depending upon my lifetime of devotion and service to keep me chained to her side. I'll never know. But there is nothing about her now that speaks to me of the love I once had for my mother, or she for her daughter. Her eyes are still cold and hard when she regards me; there is nothing left in them to remind me of the mom I once knew. Whatever has become of her, she has not awoken from her long sleep; she has not reclaimed herself from the pit into which she has fallen. Because surely she would have come to me if she were no longer sick, surely she would have sought my sympathy and my understanding. It's the only way now to tear down the ugly, thick hedge that's grown up between us, the only possible next step that could convince me that our relationship is salvageable, that it is worth saving. I know that none of this is her fault, but none of it is my fault, either. The rest of my life is too high a price to ask me to pay for her illness, and I won't pay it. I try to remember this in the years that follow, when the guilt overwhelms me for having left her. My mother left my father because he was a danger to her and her children. She took my nephew, her grandson, because he was in danger from his own mother. Undoubtedly she would want the same treatment for her daughter, too.

For some weeks now, I have been stealthily preparing, obsessively going it over again and again, the plan I have been making for more than a year. Writing out lists is out of the question, because she might find them; my plan for escape remains all in my head. Even today, I am surprised by my own readiness, my own organization. I close the P.O. Box I rented downtown to receive my secret mail. I close my bank account and keep the cash on my person; the bank book has not left my pocket since the day I reclaimed it. I give notice at the restaurant where I have been working, citing the upcoming move as my reason. I buy a used station wagon for the staggering sum of five hundred and fifty dollars, having talked down the owner from his asking price of six hundred. Even I'm not terribly impressed with the results of this negotiation, particularly when he tells me that he wouldn't drive that car across the country. It's a 1982 Dodge Aries with over one hundred thousand miles on its odometer. But I must have a means of travel, and a place to sleep, and it will have to do.

It's the car that almost ruins it, that almost kills the whole plan. It's a few days before graduation when I buy it, and since I can't very well park it in my own driveway, I hide it away on the street that curves around behind ours. Mom is beginning to be up and about on her crutches, and often hobbles to the restaurant across the street for her dinner while I am out studying or at my extra-curricular activities. Even mad and disabled, she's independent. But she is unlikely to take a casual walk around our long block, and she is not yet up to driving very far, especially not when I have her car.

Early one evening I come home and she is waiting for me. She's standing on her crutches right there in the foyer, wavering on her feet. Mom has never been much of a drinker, but nowadays when she goes out, she often has a glass or two of wine with her dinner. I hate how jolly she gets because it seems like a slap in the face of my misery. Sometimes she takes me along to keep her company while she eats, and tells me stories from her past life that may be real or not real. I don't talk at all, even though I'm grateful for the steady meals. I don't dare tell her anything in case she finds a way to use it against me. Instead I mentally measure the distance between us, making sure I'm out of reach of those crutches.

"The police were here," she informs me, audibly grinding her teeth.

Uh-oh. It's pretty easy to break the rules in this town. There's a curfew for teenagers, both for walking and driving, and technically you're not even supposed to be on school grounds after hours, which makes those nighttime visits to the elementary school playground strictly forbidden. But I'm fairly certain that I haven't done anything illegal enough to warrant a special visit home from the cops. Is this another one of her delusions returning?

"Where did you get the car?" she snaps.

I don't know whether to be scared or relieved. I'm glad that I'm not going to jail, but maybe it would be better than getting stuck back in this prison.

"What car?" I hedge.

"Don't lie to me," she hisses. "The station wagon you have parked back on the circle. It's registered to your name and this address."

Inwardly, I groan. I couldn't use my P.O. Box on the registration, or on the insurance. But of course I hadn't expected anyone to be looking at it until after I was gone.

"I bought it," I confess. Better than having her think that it's stolen.

"Why didn't you tell me?"

"I wanted to surprise you," I lie without stammering. I have never been much of a liar, but you learn quickly when your life depends upon it. "See, I, uh… It's a stick shift. I can't really drive it yet."

This is true enough. My stepfather had tried to teach me to drive a standard for two months before giving up, and I still haven't quite gotten the hang of the clutch. I'm naturally worried about it, but only slightly. It's not even in the top five of my biggest problems.

She stares at me a moment, sizing me up. I hold my breath for some seconds, mentally patting myself down. I have my keys and my wallet; I'm wearing my jacket and shoes. But even though school is effectively over, I do not have my high school diploma, and my college acceptance papers are securely locked away inside the filing cabinet I plan to take with me. Do I really need them? If she decides to attack me, should I make my break? I cannot let it all come crashing down, not now, not when the end is so temptingly near.

"You should have told me," she says at last. "I was planning to buy you a car myself, after we moved."

There's an unusual tone to her voice, a hint almost of pleading, and I stare at her, puzzled by what I am hearing. Does she really believe me? Or is this promise of a new car a token offering, some kind of bribe? Stay with me, and I'll pay for your college. Stay with me, and I'll buy you a car. But I don't need her money, and I don't want it. I don't need her to pay for my college, and I've already bought my own car. My life is my own now, and I won't sell it, at any price. But although part of me is insulted by the thought that perhaps she thinks she can buy it, another part of me is moved that she's willing to try.

"Bring it down and park it in the driveway," she orders me. "You're not allowed to park on the street in this town."

She turns and begins clumping her way across the room to the den, her steps uneven, showing that she is hurting and tired.

"I'm sorry," I call to her retreating backside.

And I am. But not about the car.

It is the day of my high school graduation. Fear churns my stomach, but hope glows in my chest. The station wagon is now parked at our house, and if my mother has plans for it, if she intends to sell it or destroy it or turn it over to one of her cop friends, she has not yet done it. In my anxious moments, I focus in on it in my mind; I picture it sitting there, waiting for me to retrieve it. Somewhere in the back of my mind I am aware that this is not the proper place for my thoughts to be, that I will have only one high school graduation, that I should try to enjoy the day for what it is and for what it should be. The other students are ranged all around me, nearly three hundred kids celebrating this special occasion with their friends and family. But for none of them is this day as special as it is for me. Graduation day is not the day that I will leave. But it is the day that sets me free.

I watch as the other students file up to accept their diplomas. Many of them I knew before my mother's illness; all of them knew me after it started. But today, that no longer matters. My part in today's ceremony will be quick and painless; the reading of my name, a hug and a handshake, and it will be done. The awards ceremony was held separately, early last week, and although I was naturally pleased to be the recipient of numerous scholarships and other honors, it embarrassed me to have to run repeatedly down the aisle in my gown and my Converse sneakers with everyone watching and staring at me. I have spent a large part of the year trying not to be seen. It will be some time yet before emotions truly begin to flood back into my psyche, but now that this ordeal is ending, I am slowly beginning to realize just how painful and life-altering it's been for me. Even if I were no longer afraid of my mother, I would still want to leave.

The ceremony ends. The students and parents are filing out of the stadium, and my mother is fumbling her way towards the car on her crutches. I must meet her shortly.

I run. The corridors are bare and the school is empty; I have only moments to return my gown and meet Jesse. I've heard a rumor that he's come home from college and is here, at the ceremony, and I'm breathless, my long white dress trailing behind me as I dash down the long, wide hallways, searching for him. I know that it is probably the last time I will ever see him. I know, too, that there isn't much time.

It's a quick and painful goodbye. We both know that Mom is waiting outside.

Were there words between us? I don't remember. This last embrace was already more than I had expected, more than I had ever hoped to get from the most important man in my life. And then I am running again, looking back at him over my shoulder long after I've left him behind.

It is six days after graduation. My mother has gone to dinner, not on her crutches, but in her own car. I am relieved that she is driving, that she can get around by herself, that she no longer needs me to take her shopping and run her errands. But I am too scared to wait; too afraid of that move to Florida to postpone it until she's fully functional. I need to go now, before she turns the house back over to my stepfather per their agreement, before she feels up to such a long drive. My graduation has freed me, but it's freed her as well. And I'm still a minor, and must go where she tells me.

But first, she'll have to find me.

For a moment I stand and look around at my disheveled room, at the half-empty closet, at the fully-made bed, now without pillows. There's no time to be sentimental, because my mother could be back any second, so I tell myself I'm only doing a last-minute check of my belongings, making sure I've left nothing behind. But of course, that's not true. I've left behind far more than I can take with me, and am taking much that I wish I could leave.

I close the door tightly behind me, wondering how much time that might buy me. How long will it be before my mother realizes that I'm not coming home, before she goes to my room to check up on me? Will she worry when I'm not back by nine, or will she figure it out the moment she sees that my car is still gone? I try not to think about how she will react, how she might feel, or even if she might feel. If she were my old mother, I would have known, would have been overly sensitive to her hurt feelings. But for so long now she has seemed to me to be an almost emotionless being, capable only of anger and rage, lacking sympathy, lacking empathy, having no capacity to feel loss or shame, no conception of the consequences of her own actions. Much later I will learn that this "flattening of emotions" is characteristic of schizophrenics[30], as is unawareness of their disease.[31] As it is, I'm not even sure she'll understand why I have left. If she could, we wouldn't be in this position.

My friends and I have finally captured the dog my mother brought home last year to guard me. He has been trained to bark loudly when I leave my room, or when anyone enters. The poor creature has been hounding us since we arrived, but he is now tied up in the yard, still barking like crazy. Our neighbors must be well aware of what's going on, but fortunately none of them seems inclined to betray me. Michelle and Karina are waiting outside in my car, in the tiny spare bit of room left in the front seat. The station wagon is packed to the brim with my belongings, tossed haphazardly inside in our hurry. I will have to repack it later if I want to lie down in the backseat.

I make the five-minute drive to Karina's and drop her off. Two minutes later, I'm at Michelle's, and I go inside to say goodbye to her folks, who have been so kind.

"Your mother just called looking for you," Michelle's father says the second we open the door. "She says she's put out an APB."

I don't know what an APB is, but I can guess what it means – that the cops are already searching for me. We must have missed my mother by merely minutes, and she must have busted open my bedroom door as soon as she got home. Perhaps she was expecting this after all.

I hug my friend very quickly, and thank her parents again for their sympathy. It's because of them that I got my scholarship, because of them that I'm even going to college. They're the ones who let me use their phone number for my Berkeley interview; the only adults in this whole fiasco that's been my young adult life to have truly helped me.

They won't tell. There isn't a soul in this town who would blame me for making a break from that house. But if the police are on their way, I'll have to hurry. I still have to reach that bold, simple sign in the road that signifies freedom.

Connecticut. I smile at it even now. I don't really know, of course, whether I can be pursued across the state line, if the local police can call ahead, stop a teenager on the run, wherever I go, wherever I am. Somehow I doubt that it's like it is in the movies or on TV, cruisers screeching back in angry frustration as I whizz past because they've lost jurisdiction. But I like to imagine it is. I like to think that if I can just make the border, that I'll be safe, that I'll be out of her reach, that no one can touch me once I'm over the line. But first, I have to get there.

From my friend Michelle's, it's only two miles. I could walk it in thirty minutes, or run it in half that, but the six minutes it takes me to drive it stretch on and on. My heart pounds as though I am running; the miles creep by as though I am walking, but I am driving, driving in this mad, twenty-mile-an-hour dash for the state line.

I have learned some lessons from the movies and television. I don't blow any stop signs or any red lights, and I don't speed. Instead I proceed carefully to the back road that's right by my house, the last place, I reason, that my mother will be looking for me. It's nearly dark, and the woods by the sides of the road are gloomy and menacing. But no men in navy blue uniforms spring out from under the trees; no Ford Crown Victorias with red-and-blue flashing lights leap out onto the pavement. No cops are waiting for me. Perhaps it's tougher to enforce an all-points bulletin when your town's entire police force consists of three cruisers.

My heart is doing somersaults inside my chest, but I can't resist looking back over my shoulder as I cross over, taking one last peek at the house where it all happened. In the twilight I can't really see more than our driveway, can't even see if my mother's car is parked in it. Is she waiting at home, or out searching for me? I feel one last pang of guilt, one last twinge of regret, but there's no going back. What might she do to me now if I did?

I almost find out. I'm in Hartford when it happens, the construction zone that's nearly my undoing. I'm in the middle of it when I lose control of the stick shift. Try as I might, the car will move only in shuddering starts and stops; I can't get it going.

"Open up!"

A policeman is banging on the driver's side window, and my heart plunges into the balls of my feet. I'm only a half-hour from home, and I've been caught already.

Maybe I could make a break for it, if I could only start the stupid car.

I roll down the window.

"What the hell is going on?" the policeman is spluttering. He catches sight of me, and his expression softens, the lines of his face losing some of their edge. Perhaps I look young; perhaps I look scared. Perhaps I look like his own teenaged daughter. "You're holding up traffic," he says, more gently.

"I'm sorry, Officer," I squeak. Please don't let him ask for my license; I cannot let him run my license! "It's the stick shift – I'm new at it – I can't get it going."

Miraculously, he doesn't ask for my license – doesn't even ask for my name. Instead, he decides to talk me through it.

"Now let up on the clutch…that's it…"

It's nothing I don't know already, but somehow it works better with his firm guidance. Before the blessed movement of tires on asphalt has even registered in my addled mind, I'm drifting back through the lane, the orange cones boldly highlighting the path that will take me away.

"And stay off the highway until you get a better handle on the stick shift!" he calls after me.

"Thank you, Officer," I yell back through the open window.

But I don't obey. I stay on I-91 all the way through Connecticut until I hit I-95, then I drive until I fall asleep at the wheel, not once but three times before I concede that I'm finished.

I see a truck stop, but I'm not a truck. Can I still stop?

I pull off the highway. Other cars are parked in the vast lot, their front seats reclined, their windows dark. I drive to a space in the rear, away from the parking lot lights. I don't have the energy to repack my space. I curl up on the front seat and go straight to sleep.

There's nothing special about the town. It's no different, perhaps, from any of the other towns I had passed through that night and morning, except that it was the one I had stopped at, landed on like a playing piece on a game board following a roll of the dice. It's warm and humid and green like every other place in New England in early summer, smelling of freshness and growing things and the perpetual threat of impending rain.

Massachusetts is gone. I've been up since before dawn, wanting to pack on more miles before daylight hits, before danger comes. And now it is morning, and the sun is shining, and I'm three states away from the state that had once been my home.

A creek runs through the meadow behind the empty office building where I've halted to rest. It sings, and it calls; it speaks to me of what it's like to be free. I bow, I kneel, I plunge into it wholeheartedly with my neck and face, washing away the sweat of fear and of running and of mid-June in the East. I cleanse myself of the unhappiness of home; leave it to be flushed away over an unnamed field on the outskirts of Cranbury, New Jersey.

No, there's nothing special about the town. Except to me.

THE INHERITANCE

I STILL RETAIN a handful of things that I brought with me from my family home. Some letters from Jesse, and a few photos. A little black dress I wore to the sophomore semi-formal with my first boyfriend; I last wore it to a wedding in 2006. A cute pair of elephant earrings that my mother bought me when I was fifteen, and the one holey tie-dyed T-shirt that's survived countless washings. The locking two-drawer filing cabinet in which I've always stored all my papers. It still holds the diary my mother gave me when I was twelve, with a lengthy letter as its inscription; it is blurred and faded beyond recognition, yet it reminds me of who she was before she got sick. My collection of books by Hermann Hesse, who was one of my favorite authors when I was a teen, and my ancient alarm clock, which still flashes the time at me in those digital squares of fire-engine red. And the necklace with the silver medallion, the yantra I bought at a New Age shop in Connecticut before I left, and which I wear around my neck to this day; it's the one piece of me that remains completely unchanged.

This is what I have left of me, and what I have left of my mother. My trinkets, my tokens, my remembrances of who I was and who I might have become.

But what did my mother have left of me?

For years I have pushed it aside, because I have had to. The guilt over leaving her. The uncertainty over whether I ought to go back. The knowledge that the pain that I must have caused was permanent, the hurt irrevocable. Yet I know, too, that she never acknowledged my hurt or my pain at all.

This is my legacy, both sides of it: the hurt that I caused, and the hurt that I felt. I've often imagined what might have happened had I stood by her. Would she have recovered? Would she have faced the reality of her mental illness, would she at last have acknowledged her sickness and what it had caused her to do? Would we have lived the rest of our lives as an ordinary mother and daughter, phoning and bickering and getting together on important occasions? Would I have consoled her on her deathbed, and wept at her passing?

Perhaps. Or perhaps it would have panned out the way I imagined it when I was sixteen, with me dead in some swamp in the Everglades, my body bloated beyond all recognition, with no one to claim it. Perhaps I would have been whisked away to Brazil, or Argentina, and would still be trying to escape the terrors of the jungle and my mother's firm grasp. Perhaps I would be chained up in some attic or cellar, tortured daily in order to force me to reveal the truth about my father, or sister, or some other imaginary enemy who was trying to kill her. These were the potential realities that I was facing. Mother or monster: which would she be?

My mother left me with no physical gifts. There were no tokens, no trinkets, no remembrances of who she was or what she might have become. Only one last letter, and long lists of questions. But perhaps she left me with the greatest gift she was able to give. She let me be. She let me live.

It would be wrong to say that I have no inheritance, because it lives inside me; I am my mother's own legacy. Her strength, her courage, her determination; I carry them with me. Her work ethic, her practical nature, her strict economy; I survived because she taught them to me.

Yet I am perhaps most grateful for the gift that she didn't give me, the one piece of her legacy that I would have refused had it been offered to me.

Who knows where she got it? There is abundant proof that there is a heritable component to schizophrenia and other mental disorders, a genetic predisposition that increases the chances of an innocent child being inflicted with the disease. Yet as far as I know, insanity did not run in my mother's family.

I can't ever know. All I can know is what she decided to tell me. So many questions without any answers. There is no one to ask.

Yet we do ask, all of us, we children of the mentally ill. We ask ourselves those unnerving, gut-wrenching questions, over and over we ask them. When did it happen? Why did it happen? How did it happen?

Will it happen to me?

Like me, Mom rarely spoke about her family, yet there were a handful of stories with which she did like to regale me. How Uncle Ernie lost a finger to a firework that went off in his hand. How her sister liked to blow through red lights at intersections by honking her horn and yelling "No brakes! No brakes!" out the car's open window. How when the children behaved badly, her mother would send them out to the yard for a switch – until they grew old enough to refuse to go fetch their own switch. How she hated getting dollar bills from Grandpa because he always insisted on tucking them into her bra.

Her stories were not always pretty or pleasant. But there were none that suggested a familial history of severe mental illness. If those stories existed, she never shared them with me.

Would Mom have told me if they did? I don't know that she would have. Look at all of the secrets she kept, for most of my youth. Consider the one she keeps still, of the half-sister I never knew, of Sandra Johnson, who is a mystery that will remain forever unsolved. My mother was raised in a generation in which mental illness was seldom discussed and even more seldom revealed, in which sufferers would often be sent away, locked up, confined to asylums, abandoned by their families, and scorned by their friends. A time in which anxiety was nervousness, depression was laziness, a breakdown was weakness.

No, it would not surprise me if she had concealed and kept silent. Most of us do. No one wants to be subjected to the evaluation and judgment, to the pernicious suspicions that are suddenly aroused when we engage in behaviors that, in any other individual, would merely be deemed eccentric. No one wants to suffer the watching and waiting, the unease of knowing that our friends and our lovers are counting the years until they can be truly assured that whatever our fears, and whatever our flaws, we are not also insane.

How could we not be eccentric? How could we not be fearful and flawed?

A condition like my mother's can be contagious in its own roundabout way. Her fears made her dangerous, which made me afraid. Her suspicions made me question what truths might lie at their roots. Her violence would threaten me for the rest of her life; her unpredictability would prevent me from feeling safe, in that natural way that normal children feel safe.

There is no cure for being the child of an unstable parent. Children learn what they are taught, and the effects last a lifetime. Yet, like many of the lessons we learn as a child, some of them fade into bare recollection. Twenty years ago I slept every night with my sneakers and a pair of jeans at my bedside, my keys in the right front pocket, my wallet in the back left. Fifteen years ago I was still carrying both beneath my gear when I went to play hockey, in spite of the bruises I'd get from poorly placed falls. In the last ten years they've moved to a jacket that I keep not in my bedroom, but on a chair in my office, and twice in the last five years I've even permitted my boyfriend to hold my purse or my keys – for a few minutes.

I know that most people don't live with this unending dread, with this need to be permanently prepared in case of attack, to be ready to spring to escape at the slam of a door or the slap of a hand. I know that I will never be the type of person who tosses their car keys casually onto a counter and forgets all about them, or who isn't sure where they've tucked their money or credit card or license to drive. I will never quite relax, or go with the flow, or allow anyone ever to take control of my cash or my body or the place I call home.

This is what I've been taught. This is what I have learned.

It is definitely not normal. But it is not mental illness.

There were, of course, times when I was younger when I wondered. Would I be able to see it coming, if it came for me? Would I recognize what was happening, if it happened to me?

I always thought that I would. Having a loved one with a serious illness makes you hyper-sensitive to the signs of that condition. I would never have disregarded a voice in my head; would never have ignored a hallucination. Even mild paranoia would have prompted me to wonder if there were a problem. Mom may not have been so completely prepared.

There was no one to tell her. My mother, like me, was nearly alone in the world, with no one to intervene, no one to notice that she was in trouble. No one to know that she was slipping, falling, drifting, drowning; even she herself may never have known.

But I knew. That role was left to me, one solitary teenage girl, watching helplessly as her last loved one went forever away. Without even saying goodbye.

.

APPENDIX

IN THE PROCESS of publishing this memoir, I have also published a number of short stories, essays, guest blog posts, and interviews related to it. This appendix features a selection of these supplemental writings.

"Bus Ride," "Hide and Seek," "Poisoned," "Found Money," and "Cranbury, New Jersey" are fictionalized versions of segments of my mother's story; as I discuss in the essay "On Writing My Memoir," it was through these that the idea of writing a memoir was born. "You Don't Have to Be Mentally Ill to Suffer from the Stigma Associated with Mental Illness" describes the social aspects of being the child of a parent who was mentally ill, while my "Author Interview with Ognian Georgiev (Excerpt)" delves into further aspects of the writing process. Finally, "The Photograph" offers the sole remaining visual representation of a captured moment from my mother's illness.

THE "I AM SUBJECT" PROJECT

I ORIGINALLY COMPOSED the following essay for Diane DeBella's "I Am Subject" project, in which she invited women to write about a moment in which they claimed or reclaimed themselves as the subjects of their own lives. It appeared in her anthology *I Am Subject: Women Awakening* in September 2014. You can learn more about the #IamSubject project at http://www.iamsubject.com/.

"On Writing My Memoir" perfectly describes my experience of creating this book. But more than that, I am including it here because I have been absolutely overwhelmed by the responses of those who have read it. So many of us, it seems, are carrying these stories of hurt, fear, and pain somewhere inside ourselves. And while our individual experiences vary, the emotions are the same. We all hurt. We all have fear. We all have pain.

But we all, too, have strength. We have power. Even the weakest and meekest among us glow and shine with the light of hope, the light of life. We try, we fight, we strive. We endure. We survive.

We are all a part of one another's stories. I thank you from my heart for sharing in mine.

ON WRITING MY MEMOIR

I FORGOT HER.

I hadn't intended it. I didn't mean to forget, or to set her aside. I didn't plan to consign her to the fog of some distant past, or to the blur of some hazy future. I had no plans for her at all. I didn't even realize that she was missing. I did not know that she had been forgotten.

About a year ago now, this young woman I had banished from my memory returned without warning. I know what prompted it. I found my mother's obituary online. She had died, without my knowing it, six years before.

My mother was gone. Her insanity and the cruelty to which it drove her would lie forever buried, vanquished by the final failure of her physical being; she would never return. But that young woman would.

She came to me first in the guise of a story. Not a memory, but a story, a short piece of fiction that bore a striking resemblance to a vague recollection I had of her life. It wasn't true. It wasn't real. How could it have been?

A short time later, she came again, with another story to tell. To quiet her, once more I put her in fiction. But I didn't examine her character closely. She couldn't bear examination, and neither could I. Still, she kept coming. She appeared before me month after month, in story after story, until suddenly I realized that her stories were no longer fiction. They had diverged unexpectedly into other forms, into nonfiction and narratives, essays and vignettes. Short bursts of truth expunged onto paper.

They meant little at first. A memory here, an incident there. Never very personal, and never very real, at least not to me. Events that had indeed transpired, but in another woman's life. Not in hers, and certainly not in mine.

I continued to write them down nonetheless. They were compelling, these bits and pieces of someone else's past. Some of them sad. Some of them frightening. But after a time it hurt, telling her stories. It was no longer merely an exercise; I began to feel it, someplace inside. Someplace I had forgotten I still kept inside.

They were horrible stories. A mother's psychosis. A daughter's terror. Stories of pain and isolation, of threats and violence. Stories of a woman who needed help and never knew it; stories of a girl who cried for help and never received it. Stories of hunger and homelessness, of the ever-present fear of capture and the deathly slow torture of starvation. Stories of a runaway shivering through cold autumn nights filled with loneliness and desolation. It pained me to tell them so I stopped. I had forgotten that girl and her stories two decades before. What sense was there in bringing them back now?

I put them away. But I could not put her away. She would not go quietly, as she had twenty years ago, when, more than anything, I had needed to leave her behind. This time she stayed; this time she waited. Until I was ready to share the rest of her story.

It happened unexpectedly one spring afternoon, just a few weeks ago, when the sun was shining brightly and a stiff breeze was blowing across the rooftop where I like to do my writing. The last six thousand words, the ones I had been holding back, the ones that told what was left of her story. Not of what had happened to her. That I had told already, the factual version, a clinical history of severe mental illness. No, these words finally revealed how I felt about it, of what it meant to me, deep down in places I don't care to explore. How sorry I am for her pain. How deeply I feel for her, that young woman whose life took such dreadful and devastating turns. How deeply I feel for me, for having to remember. For how much it hurts me to have to remember.

I found myself weeping as I typed, weeping over a long-distant past, the words blurring before my eyes as, for the first time in twenty-some years, she came sharply into focus, that girl that used to be me. How hard it is to hurt for someone else. How much harder still, to hurt for yourself.

I had tucked her away into the deepest recesses of my mind, into the darkest corners of my heart, that unfortunate young woman I once knew so well, so intimately, that I could not have distinguished between her and me. I thought I could leave her behind, as I had left my family behind; thought I could forget, get by without her.

But that day on the rooftop with the sun warming my face and the wind whipping away my tears, I knew this could not be. I had lost a vital piece of myself, of who I am and who I was. I had to reclaim her, to re-forge the connection between her and me, to integrate us, the former she and the current me.

The following day I added the final segment to my memoir. It depicts perhaps the most important part of our journey together because it's the story of our transition, from her into me. The story of how a dauntless young woman somehow managed to dig her way out of a hole of despair, to hold onto hope in a sea of hopelessness, to fight a battle she had little to no chance of winning. Because what I discovered, when I opened the door to let her back into my life, was that much of my strength lies not with me, but with her. And as I find myself facing a new set of trials I finally understand how much I need her, how firmly I must grasp hold of the young woman I used to be, for she, more than I, has the power to persevere, to overcome, to survive.

Perhaps I do not like the memories she brings. Perhaps I would prefer to allow her to settle quietly into the dust of my personal history, to let her remain forever buried, as my mother is now. But with her inside me I need not shy away from fear, from pain. She copes with fear. She handles pain. She is, and always has been, subject.

I cannot be subject without her. But together, we can be.

THE PHOTOGRAPH

IT IS IN one of the in-between times, when Mom has decided to let me out for a while. Perhaps she has grown fearful of Social Services. Perhaps she intends to inspect the house from roots to rafters and wants me out of the way. Perhaps she's simply sick of watching me all day and all night. I don't know. I know better than to question it.

My friends and I are at a hotel for a school function of some sort. I don't remember exactly why. Band, or perhaps Key Club? It doesn't matter. I have reached a point where nothing seems very real.

I am wearing an orange dress my mother bought me. It's hideous, but I don't realize that until later. Jesse is with me. He is holding me. I am grateful.

We are on one of the upper floors. We are beside a railing. It overlooks the center of the hotel. We are talking. I don't know what about.

I can see us standing there together. Me in that ugly orange dress with my hair cut short, my face buried in his shoulder. Him with his arms wrapped in a circle around me. I can see it, see it as if I'm above it and not inside it, and in my mind I've gotten up onto the railing and I'm teetering there, on the verge of going over, and I don't know how to stop it; don't know if I even care anymore about trying to stop it.

"Lori," Jesse whispers, clutching me tighter. "Lori, I think you're going insane."

After completing my memoir, I inquired of some of my high school friends whether they had in their possession any photos I might be able to use in assembling my book trailer. Imagine my reaction when my friend Ben – who was always the big picture-taker of the group – responded with this photograph:

Stunned and happy and heartbroken. To see that moment, captured forever on film, somehow makes it all the more devastating, all the more real. The picture can't tell what we were saying or thinking. Yet somehow it does. Somehow, it does.

YOU DON'T HAVE TO BE MENTALLY ILL TO SUFFER FROM THE STIGMA ASSOCIATED WITH MENTAL ILLNESS

WHEN STIGMA FIGHTERS first asked me to write a guest post, I refused them. The goal of their site is to end the stigma associated with mental illness by bringing it out into the open, and their writers are usually people with depression or anxiety or bipolar disorder. Upon further discussion with the publisher of the site, however, it occurred to me that I was actually in a prime position to understand this stigma, because I had experienced it from a different angle – that of a child of mental illness. All my life, I have been a victim of stigma without even being mentally ill!

I strongly support treating mental disorders as biological illnesses, which is what they are. The perverse thinking that the mentally ill are somehow weak or deformed or defective is of no help to patients, to society, or to friends and families; it is also cruel to our fellow humans, and serves no useful purpose to those of us who are not sick.

You don't have to be mentally ill to suffer the stigma of mental illness.

I know all about it. My mother became psychotic when I was a teenager. She may never have known how the world saw her – or me – after she got sick. But I did.

You can imagine what it was like, living in a small town with a parent with a severe mental illness. There probably wasn't anyone who didn't know. My mother's delusions didn't permit her to sit quietly at home where no one would notice her sickness. She believed that someone was waiting to attack me at school, and at length she somehow persuaded the school board to allow her to attend classes with me.

You can fault her actions, but you can't fault her motives. Besides, at the time, I considered it an improvement. Prior to that, she had removed me from school completely.

It sounds almost funny, more than twenty years later. In reality, of course, few things could have been more humiliating than being "that girl with the crazy mother." There was something very strange about meeting someone after class – every class – and having it be my own mother. There was something even more bizarre about being confronted by snickering strangers in those rare moments when I found myself alone.

"Hey, aren't you that girl whose mother has green hair and comes to school with her?"

"It isn't really green," I would argue. "It's supposed to be blonde; something just went wrong with the coloring."

Yet this was how I would forever after be known. Until the day I ran away from home, that's who I was: Judy Green-Hair's daughter. To certain people, I probably always will be.

That was the flip side of it. Even people who cared about me began to treat me differently because of what had happened to my mother. Some of my friends became cautious in dealing with me; many of their parents, much more so. Their attitude wasn't unreasonable. My mother was dangerous and unpredictable; it was only natural for people to want to avoid her, even when that meant avoiding me.

It is also true that a predilection for mental illness is often hereditary, and can be passed down through the generations. Therefore it also wasn't completely unreasonable for them to wonder whether I, too, might one day succumb to my mother's affliction.

I understood this. Still, I very quickly tired of having my every move, my every action evaluated and reevaluated, as if everything I did might serve as confirmation that I, too, had lost control of my mind.

My experience of adolescence was anything but ordinary. But in many ways, I was still an average teenager who did average – and stupid – teenage things. When my mother had operations on her feet in my senior year, she was housebound for several months. It was the first taste of freedom I'd experienced in quite some time, and I acted accordingly. I snuck out at night. I skipped classes to hang out with my friends. I drank and made an ass of myself. I did dumb things that I regretted. Who doesn't?

In any other teenager, these types of behaviors would have been considered normal acts of rebellion. But not for me. No, when I did it, it was evidence. Was I sane, or insane?

For example, when I finally got to college, I experimented with drugs. Nothing hard-core; nothing out of the ordinary for a kid who was on her own for the first time. I happened to mention this to a friend of mine from back home in a letter. Someone who, incidentally, had already done far more experimenting then I had ever done, or ever would do.

I could not have been more stunned by his response. He inscribed to me a lengthy lecture regarding many aspects of my behavior in recent years, and cautioned me strongly against using any more recreational substances.

"How could you be so stupid? What if that was what drove your mother insane?"

I was so angry that I responded with a letter containing the return address of an insane asylum and a detailed description of how my basket-weaving courses were going.

The last laugh was on me, however. Seems people were so ready to believe that I had gone off my rocker that they entirely missed the sarcasm of my missive. In return, I received delicately worded responses from other friends wishing me a speedy recovery.

My mother's condition is not something I've advertised over the years. It's hard to explain something like that. And it's usually better not even to try.

Because people do think of you differently, when they know you're a child of someone who was mentally ill. Consider my circumstances. My mother was violent and irrational. I lived in a state of constant fear, and after I left home, I lived in my car and couldn't afford to eat. Expecting me to be happy and well-adjusted? Now that would be crazy! Yet no one ever looked at me and said, "All things considered, she's doing well."

All things considered, I was doing well. I made my own way in the world without any help from anyone – which is an achievement of which none of my "sane" friends can ever boast.

Yet there were still those who breathed a sigh of relief when I got to be old enough where it was unlikely that I would turn out to be schizophrenic. All those years of watching, waiting, and evaluating had finally drawn to an end.

I can't guess what it's like truly to be mentally ill. But I do know how the world treats those that are, and it isn't pretty. In fact, it's precisely why people like my mother never get treatment. Who would ever want to admit that they had a problem if they knew how harshly they were going to be judged for it?

My mother died in 2007. I no longer have to equivocate when people ask me about her.

"She's dead," I say simply.

People are sorry. I suppose that's nice, that they're sorry that my mother is gone.

But why wasn't anyone ever sorry when I said she was ill?

BUS RIDE

"HOW WOULD YOU like to take a ride on a bus, Gloria?" her mother said cheerfully, her eyes twinkling in expectation of her daughter's delighted response.

She wasn't disappointed. "A real bus?" Gloria squealed. "I've never ridden on a bus before!"

"I know you haven't," her mother confirmed. "But today we're going to."

"How come?" Gloria wondered, puzzled. "Why aren't we taking the car?"

"Because... because where we're going, it's better to go by bus."

"Where are we going?" Gloria replied, her enthusiasm rebounding.

"It's a surprise," her mother answered, glancing around their high-ceilinged foyer and putting a finger to her lips as if afraid that the secret might leak out. "Now go and get ready."

Gloria eagerly fetched her pink windbreaker and wiggled into her tennis shoes, struggling only slightly with the plastic-tipped laces before feeling confident that they were properly secured. Her mother stood waiting by the door, a small satchel no bulkier than a large purse on her shoulder, a light jacket on her arm.

They walked. Around corner after corner they stepped silently, Gloria's mother grasping Gloria's hand tightly and keeping her reined in upon the sidewalks, away from the curbs and busy streets of town. The mounting sun warmed their shoulders as morning gave way to nearly noon, and Gloria understood why they'd never ridden the bus before; it was a long walk to the stop.

At last they arrived. She still thought it strange that they hadn't taken the car, but she soon forgot about that, watching the other

132

people waiting. The hunchbacked old man perched on the bench, resting his elbow on a wooden cane. The young woman pacing, consulting her watch every few steps, worrying that she'd be late. The sandy-haired man with the glasses, a baby peacefully asleep in his arms, a stroller and diaper bag crowded about his feet while he rocked in steady rhythm.

The bus finally appeared, its square face wobbling over the cracks and ridges in the asphalt as it approached. Gloria wanted to shout, but her mother shushed her, pointing to the sleeping child, and she immediately fell silent. She watched with interest as the passengers boarded, then followed them awkwardly up the precipitous steps. Taking the coins her mother handed her, she plunked them, one by one, into the canister, where they rang out gleefully as if pleased with their gleaming new home. She trailed along behind her mother, passing more strangers, faces she barely had a chance to glimpse before moving on, to the very back of the bus, the last two seats at the rear. She sat down on the aisle and peered shyly up it while her mother settled into the seat beside her. Glancing around, she saw the backs of the heads of her fellow bus-riders, light and dark and tall and short. She heard the baby wake, chortle, and fall back into sleep. Smelled the powerful perfume of the dignified-looking lady across the aisle. Felt the vibration of the floor change as the engine struggled up hills and around turns, and change again when they descended or straightened. She stared as passengers stood, grasped the cord to ring the bell, then disembarked at mysterious destinations. One by one they lumbered down the steps, blinking their eyes against the sudden sunshine before hurrying off down the street to their home or their job or their hobby or haven.

And still they rode. The passengers had become boring, repetitive; Gloria, like her mother, gazed silently out the window instead. The stops became infrequent and the city grew sparse, dissolving into suburbs, farms, pastures; wide-open spaces where it was hard to imagine that people really lived.

Only the two of them remained now. Gloria gazed out over the bold yellow field that ran alongside the road and perceived, just beyond the next curve, a dusty crossroads transecting their path. The bus crawled to a halt shortly before they reached it, and Gloria's attention was aroused anew; they hadn't rung the bell.

The driver was approaching them. A stooped middle-aged man

with a dented nose, a smattering of white hairs in his neatly trimmed beard, and a well-pressed navy-blue uniform. Gloria had barely noticed him in her excitement over the coin-taking machine.

"Ma'am?" he said politely to Gloria's mother. "Don't you want to get off here?"

"No, thank you," her mother answered in a timid, squeaky voice, a tone that Gloria had never heard her use before.

"Ma'am," he repeated. "Ma'am, you have to get off here, do you understand? This is the end of the line."

"The end of the line?" she repeated, confused.

He nodded, gesturing sideways with his elbow as if pointing her in the direction of the open, waiting door.

She hesitated and faced Gloria, who looked back with wonder.

"I guess we'll have to get off here, sweetheart," she said, enfolding her daughter's delicate hand in her own moist and quivering palm.

Gloria stumbled down the formidable steps and emerged, like the other passengers, blinking blindly against the brilliant sunshine. She watched through watering eyes as the bus turned and began retreating slowly back towards the town. Her mother stood watching it, too.

"Where are we going, Mom?" she pleaded.

"I told you, dear; it's a surprise," her mother reassured her as she surveyed the landscape with anxious, probing eyes.

"But do you know where it is?" Gloria inquired, inexplicably feeling as though she wanted to cry.

"Of course I do! I'm just not sure exactly... how to get there," she confessed, her lip trembling as if she, too, was holding back tears.

Gloria gazed up at her mother. Felt the squeeze of her hand; saw the fear in her face. Saw it and took it for her own.

"But when are we going to get there, Mom?" she whimpered.

"Soon, I promise you, honey. Soon."

She tugged on her daughter's thin arm, pointed her face westward, and began walking purposefully across the gleaming golden field.

HIDE AND SEEK

SHE WOKE EARLY-EARLY, in the crack that came even before dawn, in the cold that still shivered and whitened the ground, the trees, her mittenless hands.

Her mother was shaking her gently, rousing her from the deep, serene slumber that only children know. "Time to wake up, Gloria," she whispered, her voice cracking like the morning ice on a late autumn pond.

Gloria woke, then woke more. Scrutinized the dark, unfamiliar street, her unknown surroundings; searched for her comfy warm bed and failed to find it.

"Where are we?" she yawned, her exhaled breath warming her stiff upraised hand and sleepy fingers.

"Around the corner from Grandma's house," her mother murmured.

"Is that where we're going for Thanksgiving?" Gloria inquired, reviving slightly.

Her mother hesitated, her expression masked by the crisp, cold remnants of blue-black night. "Yes," she said at last. "Now get out of the car."

Gloria did what she was told. She climbed out of the car into the even colder not-quite-morning air, zipped her jacket up to her neck, and let the steel door fall shut behind her, clanging in the silence of a world still sound and fast asleep.

"Shhh!!" her mother scolded, tugging her sleeve and leading her down the hushed, frosted street.

The house loomed before them, not friendly and welcoming as when Grandma stood laughing on its front porch, waving them cheerily inside, but dark and silent and lonely, its gables deepening

135

the shadows that thickened about its entrance.

"Grandma's still sleeping," Gloria's mother whispered, tightening the thick collar of her own fleece-lined coat about her ears and neck. "So we have to be very, very quiet."

Gloria wondered why they had come so early, if Grandma wasn't awake yet. Were they going to surprise her? Prepare the turkey and place it in the oven before breakfast? But they were approaching the threshold of Grandma's heavy wooden front door, and she didn't dare speak.

Gloria's mother reached down to the worn mat which welcomed them and retrieved a key from beneath its rubbery surface. She put a finger to her lips to warn her daughter to keep quiet and cautiously creaked open the door, holding her own breath as if to silence its squeaky protest. And then returned the key to its poorly disguised small-town hiding place and beckoned Gloria inside.

Gloria followed, her eyes focused on the plaid-patterned linoleum of the foyer, the flat yellow glow of her mother's handheld flashlight, the path it dimly illuminated before her sneakered feet. Her spirits rose as they painstakingly descended the plush-carpeted stairs leading down to the basement. She loved Grandma's basement: the exquisitely carved table where she served dinner for company and holidays, the merrily crackling fireplace beneath the stone mantle, the cozy plush armchairs tucked into its corners.

"This way, Gloria," her mother murmured, guiding her away from the comfortable heart of the room, the book-lined shelves that gave it the hush of a library. Directed her instead towards the wide double-doors of the large coat closet perched in near-obscurity behind the staircase.

Gloria waited, confused, while her mother very slowly, very carefully slid open one of the white-painted doors. Why was she going in there? Grandma only used this closet for storage, for coats that were too fancy for everyday wear; the regular coat closet was upstairs. Was there something in there that she needed?

"Get in," her mother said, pointing inside, casting a thin pale circle of yellowish light with her flash. Gloria hesitated, wondering whether she'd heard the curious command correctly.

"Now, Gloria," her mother prompted sternly, her long, delicate fingernails clutched upon the edge of the door, her face obscured in the thick shadows of this strange underworld.

136

Gloria obeyed. She stepped reluctantly inside and found herself pushed up against a sea of cloth smelling faintly of mothballs and cedar, struggling with the dense pressure of the heavy coats on her meager neck and shoulders.

Her mother forcibly shoved the cloaks aside, creating a narrow rift in the wall of wool and sturdy wooden hangers. "Sit," she ordered, her voice dropping again to just above a whisper.

Gloria sat, bunched her knees clumsily up to her chest, pressed them against her own puffy, sky-blue winter jacket, and gazed querulously out at the darkened scene laid out before her: the bare table, the empty fireplace, the inaccessible armchairs.

Then her mother got in, too, sliding the door very slowly, very quietly behind her, shutting out the dim, ill-defined outline of the fat volumes lining Grandma's shelves. She joined Gloria cross-legged on the closet floor, winking off the light of her lamp as she did so.

"What are we doing here, Mom?" Gloria whispered.

Her mother swallowed uncomfortably, but there was no uncertainty in her voice when she answered. She found her daughter's frail hand with her hale one in the darkness and squeezed it lovingly, the stiff nails kept carefully in check so as not to scratch or scrape the soft, young skin. "You'll see, sweetheart. For now I just need you to be very good and very quiet."

She did her best to behave. It was almost even fun for a while, like a really good game of hide-and-seek that she would surely win if she didn't give herself away. She hugged her knees and watched through the crack between the two thin sliding portals as the light in the room grew, filtering in through the dust-covered half-windows that periodically interrupted the walls near the ceiling. Listened to the brisk footfalls and clanging noises overhead that meant Grandma was awake and making Thanksgiving. Muffled the fierce rumbling of her stomach with her hands as breakfast-time came and went and lunchtime approached. Nodded her head in weariness and in response to her mother's occasional soundless queries: sleeve-pulling and elbow-nudges. But then forgot herself and lurched from her seat when she heard, and then felt, heavy footsteps descending the stairs.

"Look, there's Daddy!" Gloria nearly cried, spotting his familiar striped sweater, his wispy whiskers through the chink between the doors. She caught herself in time and whispered it instead. "And Grandma, too!"

"Hush, child," her mother murmured back. "Do you want them to hear us?"

Gloria dropped her voice further; lowered it from a whisper to a breath. She blew the wistful words directly into her mother's waiting ear.

"Why can't we?"

She felt her mother's grip upon her hand tighten, but she didn't speak; simply sat motionless, her enigmatic eyes focused on the slender crack in the wood.

Gloria fell silent, too, disappointed, but glad they could see Daddy even if they couldn't talk to him. She hadn't seen him in weeks, ever since he had gone to stay with Grandma, who was very sick, her mother had said.

She seemed better now, Gloria thought, blinking her tired eyes against the dimness, the eerie stillness of their enclosure, gazing happily at Grandma, ornamented as usual with her fancy Christmas brooch, her hand-knit holiday scarf, lacking only the customary jolly smile with which she always greeted her favorite grandchild. She was bustling about as energetically as ever, laying her best china down on the table, fussing with the fancy napkin-rings and ornate centerpieces. Maybe that meant Daddy could come home soon.

He was clambering up and down the stairs, transporting additional padded chairs for the two tables, his gray-and-black-peppered hair disheveled, his cheeks red, puffing with the effort as he did when Gloria cried, "Carry me, Daddy!" after a gloriously long day of playing hide-and-seek in the park. He carried with him a warm breeze from the busy double-oven upstairs and a multitude of wonderful smells: Thanksgiving smells. The delicious scent of banana bread baking wafted its way into the closet, making Gloria's empty stomach ache. It was growing tiresome, being in there. She had long ago removed her jacket but the air was still stuffy and too warm and there wasn't enough room; she couldn't get comfortable with all of the coats in the way.

"How long do we have to stay here?" Gloria grumbled.

"As long as it takes," her mother murmured in response.

"But what are we waiting for? Why can't we...?" Her voice trailed off into a whimper. She couldn't help it; it swelled through her in a rush and she sniveled. The adventure was over, the game wasn't fun anymore. She knew it now, they weren't going to spring out and yell surprise; see Daddy and Grandma leap with excitement and joy. She'd been crouching in this dark, stuffy closet for hours already and she was hungry and she didn't understand why they were hiding, why they couldn't go to Thanksgiving and eat marshmallow yams and jellied cranberry sauce and pumpkin pie like they always had before.

The tears fell, wetting the clammy hand that had clasped itself firmly over her trembling mouth. She turned towards her mother, saw the narrow ray of light emanating from the dining room chandelier reflected in the whites of her eyes. Noted how it pierced and illuminated her dark pupils, gave them both hollowness and fire.

"Someone is after us, Gloria," she said somberly. "Someone very bad. Someone… who wants to hurt us. Do you understand?"

Gloria shook her head weakly, and her mother released her. "Who would want to hurt us?" she moaned.

Her mother directed her gaze back out towards the room, where Gloria's father sat perusing the newspaper, tracing circles forlornly with his foot on the thick, piled carpet, sighing as he glanced over at the kiddie table, set for one less child this year.

"That's what I'm trying to find out," her mother replied.

Gloria surrendered; stopped trying to understand it. She shifted position, unbent her knees and crossed her legs, leaned back against the long woolen coat that hugged and softened the hard wall behind her, then watched as her mother did the same. Settled quietly beside her, resolved to emulate her endurance and resignation, admire her calm commitment to her incomprehensible cause. Bold and alert, silent and stiff, she prepared to wait out the hidden holiday, the prolonged, bitter hours until Thanksgiving was over.

POISONED

"TELL THEM WHAT you gave me, sweetheart," she prompted encouragingly, referring, perhaps, to a pair of earrings, a bouquet of flowers.

"What I gave you?" he replied, puzzled.

Lately she often said and did things that he did not understand. At first he had thought it was merely nerves. She was anxious by nature, becoming agitated in heavy traffic, on dark corners, in crowded shops. When she'd refused to answer the door for the mail carrier, he'd supposed she had been spooked by one of those creepy documentary crime shows that she liked to watch.

"You know what I mean," she asserted, her glassy green eyes sliding over his.

"I'm afraid I don't." Utterly bewildered now, he leaned over to reach for her quaking hand and then withdrew when she retreated, balking at his touch.

He'd even been entertained when she'd begun naming those who might be after her.

"The president of the PTA wants to kill me," she'd declared in her now-deadpan voice.

He'd chuckled. "And why would she want to do that?"

"Several years ago I made fun of a blouse she was wearing. She's never forgotten it."

The anecdote seemed less amusing now.

"Please, honey," she urged. "You won't get into any trouble. I'm not even angry. I'm sure you didn't really mean to hurt me. Just please tell them; tell them now, before it's too late."

He should have insisted, that day last week when he'd come home from work to find her punching holes in the kitchen ceiling with a tire iron.

"What the hell are you doing?!!" he'd cried, coughing as he inhaled a cloud of dust and insulation.

"My father's hiding in the crawlspace. I don't know what he's planning."

"Your father's dead, Sheila."

"I never saw his body. Did you? You know how he hated me. He always hated me."

And now they were here, confined to this sparkling white room, surrounded by the infernal flashing and beeping of ominous machinery. The culmination of the nightmare of today. The chest pains, the shortness of breath, the terrible headache, all seemingly without cause. A panic attack, he'd suspected. Had diligently driven her to the hospital, just in case. But this…he hadn't expected this.

"I'm sorry, sweetheart," he answered at last, peering sadly into her hollow eyes. "I really don't know what you're talking about."

She sighed and let her head droop gently back upon the pillow, her scraggly chestnut hair splayed in disarray about her elongated face and neck.

After the kitchen incident, he'd gently suggested that she seek help. Mental help.

"Lots of people go to psychiatrists, honey," he'd reassured her. "I just hate to see you so worried all the time."

"I'll think it over, Tom," she'd replied with such sweet reasonableness that he'd let the matter drop, convinced that she'd come around of her own volition.

She was rousing again, as if in response to his thoughts; was leaning towards him, her eyes meeting his, suddenly blinking with tenderness, recognition of the man she called husband. She held out a single shivering hand, palm up and open, in gesture almost of believing, of welcome, of reaching out to him with hands and heart. "Tom," she said quietly, with feeling, and his heart leapt, while his hand, too, leapt forward to take hold of her, to pull her from the depths over which she was so precariously poised, to cling desperately, intently to her; mind, body and soul.

She jerked suddenly away, tore herself from the proffered handhold, and grasped instead the wire secured to her chest. Slowly she turned to face her attendants. "He's not going to admit it, is he?" she mused dolefully, seeking pity in the eyes of the hovering physician, the wide-eyed nurse, and then lapsing into an exhausted, anguished, waking dream.

Tom gazed longingly at her, the woman he had so lately loved, who had so lately loved him. Wept as she transformed before him, her eyes falling out of focus, no longer seeing the world around them but a hidden, more frightening one within. Watched his wife journey to a place where he could never join her, a place where she would live alone now; a place without him.

This piece was inspired by an incident that occurred in the course of my mother's mental illness. One day she took me to the hospital, complaining of chest and abdominal pains. I was naturally concerned, but I also recall being hopeful that having a doctor examine her would lead to the (I thought) inevitable revelation that she'd lost her marbles. No such luck. But they did take her complaints seriously, because although she was in fairly good health, at forty-one she wasn't exactly young anymore, and was a smoker besides, so there was legitimate reason to believe there could be a problem with her heart. They gave her the requisite battery of tests, but couldn't find anything wrong. Now, as an adult, I can guess what they must have told her – that she'd had an anxiety attack, which she probably had – but at the time, of course, I had no idea such a thing even existed. In fact, as she was imagining a lot of strange things in those days, I was more inclined to believe that her heartache was all in her head. But then the doctor left the room and the interrogation began. And that's when I began to be afraid that she'd somehow manage to pin the blame on me for her mysterious illness...

FOUND MONEY

A FIVE-DOLLAR BILL. Fluttering there on the sidewalk, yet miraculously motionless in the early-morning breeze; flapping just enough to attract her attention without flying away.

Her foot clamped down upon it, hard. She squatted down fast and dug it out with greedy fingers, then crushed it into a ball and stuffed it deep in her pocket.

It was barely past dawn. Nothing was open. Lila wondered who had dropped it, who had been benign or foolish enough to toss away five whole dollars as if it were nothing, as if it meant nothing. Ah, well, he or she would be thinking in self-consolation. It's only five dollars. It's not life or death.

She glanced at the barricaded door. The curtains hadn't been drawn yet, but the familiar sign still stood in the window. Breakfast, two dollars. Coffee, eggs and toast. She almost smiled. She sat down on the sidewalk, waiting. It smelled of stale vomit. It wasn't hers, she knew. She'd been down the road a ways when her last meal had come up on her.

There was a click and the door opened behind her. She jumped up and ran inside without speaking. She laid the bill conspicuously on the counter so they would know she had the money. They were very kind. They brought her extra coffee and packets of jelly that she ate plain when she ran out of toast.

It lasted longer this time, and it stayed down longer, too. But she was sorry because it came up right next to the library where she liked to spend the rainy days. Still, it was something, wasn't it? Finding five dollars. Not a matter of life or death, maybe. Not just yet.

What's conspicuously and intentionally absent from this piece is any kind of emotion. I don't think you can afford to have feelings when you're quite literally starving, and during most of this period in my life, it's safe to say that the emotional part of my mind was effectively switched off. But I cried when I found that money. Oh, how I cried.

I will never forget the people in that restaurant, either. They only spoke to one another in Chinese, so I have no idea what they said about me, if they said anything. But they went out of their way to be kind to someone who was obviously homeless, and probably very dirty and smelly, and that touched me deeply.

That day marked a turning point in my young life. Not because I found five dollars; a loaf of bread and a small jar of peanut butter later, it was gone. The more important thing I found on the sidewalk that day was something I hadn't even realized I'd lost. Hope.

CRANBURY, NEW JERSEY

NOTHING SPECIAL ABOUT the town. It was no different, perhaps, than any of the other towns she'd passed through that night and morning, except that it was the one that she'd stopped at, landed on like a playing piece on a game board following a roll of the dice. Warm and humid and green like every other place in New England in early summer, smelling of freshness and growing things and the perpetual threat of impending rain.

Massachusetts was gone. She'd driven as long as she could before insurmountable sleepiness had forced her to exit at that truck stop and nap in the unlit rear corner of its parking lot. Had gotten up while it was still dark and continued on, packing on miles before daylight hit, before danger came.

It hadn't gone off well. They'd only had an hour to get it done, Lila and the friend who had helped her haphazardly throw her things into the back of the car she'd bought in secret. The dog her mother had adopted to spy on her had escaped, nipping and clawing at their heels until they'd chased it down, corralled it back into the house, into the bedroom where it was accustomed to keeping watch, to barking loudly if she made a move in the middle of the night. Their time had run short; her mother had returned home to find her gone and was on the phone with her friend's father before Lila had even finished saying goodbye.

He wouldn't tell. There wasn't a soul in town who would blame her for making a break from that house. But the police were on their way and she'd had to hurry, two miles through town to that bold, simple sign in the road that signified freedom.

Connecticut. She smiled at it now. She didn't really know, of course, whether she could be pursued across state lines. If the local

145

police could call ahead, stop a teenager on the run, wherever she was, wherever she went. But she liked to imagine it so: cruisers screeching back in angry frustration as she whizzed past them over the border.

It was the highway construction zone that had nearly betrayed her; almost wrecked her escape. The series of shuddered starts and stops a dead giveaway of one who was unaccustomed to a manual transmission. A police officer had approached her window, banged angrily upon it. Softened when she'd opened up. Examined her license. Advised her to stay off the highway until she got a better handle on the stick shift. And then let her go.

Let her go, three states away from where she had once called home.

A creek ran through the meadow back of the empty office building where she had halted again to rest. She knelt, plunged into it face-first, washed away the sweat of fear and running and mid-June in the East. Cleansed herself of the unhappiness of home; left it to be flushed away over an unnamed field on the outskirts of Cranbury, New Jersey.

AUTHOR INTERVIEW
WITH OGNIAN GEORGIEV (EXCERPT)

Q. WHAT IS YOUR book about?

A. *On Hearing of My Mother's Death Six Years After It Happened* commemorates my adolescent experience of my mother's psychosis. I was sixteen when it happened, and I watched helplessly as she became violent and dangerous, to the point where I literally feared for my life. Her fears and delusions grew so powerful that for a time she took me out of our house, and even out of school. After several botched attempts at escape, I finally succeeded in running away from home just a week after graduation, only to find myself facing months of homelessness and hunger – and the ever-present fear of her tracking me down again.

Q. How did you decide to write the story?

A. The book actually came about almost by accident. After I completed my first novel, I rapidly discovered that no publisher was going to look at it if I had no other publishing credits to my name. So I began composing short works – flash fiction, short stories, essays – any idea that came into my head, I wrote something about it. Naturally, a number of those ideas were inspired by this incredibly trying period in my life.

Still, I had no intention of making anything of the story until May of 2013, when I quite coincidentally discovered my mother's obituary online while doing a search for myself. That was when I learned that she had died – in 2007. Needless to say, this brought those painful memories nearer to the forefront of my mind, and several months later, when I had amassed nearly thirty publishing credits and was ready to start submitting to publishers again, I reviewed my body of short work and discovered that I had nearly enough material about my mother to form a book. It was at that point that I decided to assemble the individual stories and tie them together into one connected work.

Q. What was the biggest challenge during the write up process?

A. The biggest challenge was – and still is – dealing with emotions that I buried somewhere inside me years and years ago. To a certain extent, I'm able to remember the things that happened to me in a clinical fashion – objectively, as if they're someone else's story. After I completed what I thought was the final draft of the book – which was about half the length it is now – I set it aside for a few months, as I always do, so that I could give it one last edit before finalizing it. When I went back to it, I realized that it was missing something, something rather important. Emotion. The story that I had written was interesting and compelling, but it lacked any real feeling. I had no trouble describing the events of my youth – but I hadn't permitted myself to remember how I felt about them.

If it weren't for the book, I don't think I would have dug any deeper. It's been very upsetting to me on a personal level, and I'm frankly not convinced that forcing myself to relive past traumas has been beneficial to my emotional health. Yet I realized that, to succeed as a memoir, the story needed it. Because, of course, a memoir isn't just for the writer; it's for the reader. Maybe I know how I felt, but readers can't know unless I tell them. I had to force myself into a place where I could communicate those experiences as more than just an objective observer, and I found that very painful. I shed a lot of tears, more than I've cried in years. It was worth it in the end, though. I even wrote an essay about the process, which I've included in the book; it was featured in Diane DeBella's *I Am Subject* anthology. The overwhelmingly positive responses I've gotten from readers who have read the essay and been inspired to share their own stories because of it convinced me that it was the right thing to do.

Q. Tell us something more about the main characters? Are they all taken from your real life?

A. The main characters are my mother and I, and yes, I've sought to portray us as we really were during this time. In addition, I've attempted to reconstruct events as accurately as I can, but the fact is, I simply don't recall every detail. This is one of the reasons I composed the narrative in fragments – this allowed me to skip over pieces that are missing from my recollection and focus only on those I remember vividly and well.

There were a handful of other individuals who were tangentially involved in our story, and although I've changed all of their names in order to respect their privacy, I've also made them as true-to-life as possible. Anyone who knew me back then would recognize the real-life characters for who they were – I didn't use composites in any way. Interesting side note, however – quite a lot of the information I obtained about some of the people in the story was through my mother, who was, at this point in time, highly delusional. I've therefore sometimes wondered about the reliability of statements she made about my sister, or my stepfather, for instance. I've attempted to convey these doubts at appropriate intervals in my memoir.

Q. How much time did you need to finish the story and to publish it?

A. I couldn't even guess. About half of it I wrote in segments, as individual short stories and essays, without having any notion of eventually compiling them into one connected work. I wrote the first set of transitional sections over a few weeks, then the last few some months later. All told, I guess it took about eighteen months – during which time I also completed a full-length novel and got halfway through drafting two more! I guess you could safely say it was not my fastest moving project.

OTHER BOOKS BY THE AUTHOR

IT'S THE IRON: HOW MY IRON DEFICIENCY ANEMIA WAS MISDIAGNOSED AS ARTHRITIS, AND WHY YOUR DEPRESSION, FIBROMYALGIA, ANXIETY, AND CHRONIC PAIN AND FATIGUE MIGHT BE LOW IRON, TOO

PAIN

IT PRESSES, PULLS, binds. Stretches like elastic from her hip to her foot; tugs hard, yanks on her muscles like a new rubber band, fresh and springy from a box on the shelf. Or threatens to snap like an old one, dug from the depths of a drawer, cracking and fraying; no longer secure enough to hold anything worth saving.

It reaches, up from between her shoulder-blades and around her neck; extends its filthy feelers in clawing fingers about her skull, around her eyes. It never prickles but she wishes it would; prickling would signify transition, a waking from pain into painlessness, from painful to pain-free. Instead there is only pain or no pain, and as time passes, much less of the latter.

It penetrates, permeates, confines. Settles deep in each crevice, in every nook of her body, every place that was designed to turn or bend or crook, even when she is not turning or bending or crooking. Mangles her thumbs and each individual toe; causes her grip upon it to falter, fail; her mastery over its power to quaver and quail.

She rolls and it shifts, moves, settles into a new groove, like a thick blanket draped heavily over delicate curves, conforming deliberately to an altered shape, a rough-hewn landscape of juts and joints. But it doesn't dissipate, doesn't lessen; only changes its

150

position, its points of attack. Its well-trained forces advance and retreat in tandem, numbers undiminished, unharmed by the battle; regrouping, reforming. Gathering strength before middle-age has dared to strike; before youth has even had time to fly.

But she flies. Cautiously plots her escapes, chooses her moments; those in which even temporary liberty is worth the price of pain. She leaps, jumps, runs away from it, runs hard; hard enough even to outpace it, to leave it behind in her bed, her chair, the carpet on which she sometimes lays, when rising only drains and exhausts. It is surprised, staved off, defenseless against the fresh bold blood coursing swiftly through a perfect, pristine body, and she will be free of it for a time: half a day, half a shift, half an hour. Half a minute before it returns, even more powerful than before; more powerful than ever before.

It persuades. Grasps her legs and binds them, weights them; converts the run into a walk and the walk into a shuffle. A shuffle that one day itself may no longer be; may devolve into a sit, a lay, a position of less pain and then at last, again, more pain. Pain ever-increasing, ever-stronger, ever-fuller. Pain evermore.

I wrote this essay in 2013 in an attempt to describe what was happening to me. It conveyed my pain in ways that a mere clinical description of it could not. It wasn't until 2016 that I discovered that the "arthritis" that had completely taken over my life was not arthritis at all, but something much simpler, much more benign. All of this pain had been for nothing. How many people besides me are suffering needlessly from this horrible pain?

It was then that I began my research. And what I discovered was truly shocking...

Hundreds of millions of people worldwide are struggling with diagnoses of debilitating and difficult-to-treat disorders such as arthritis, depression, fibromyalgia, and chronic pain and fatigue. Many of them, however, do not actually have these life-altering conditions. They are suffering from low iron, a highly treatable nutrient deficiency that, if corrected, would entirely eliminate their pain and depressive symptoms. Sadly, most of them will never know it.

It's the Iron: How My Iron Deficiency Anemia Was Misdiagnosed as Arthritis, and Why Your Depression, Fibromyalgia, Anxiety, and Chronic Pain and Fatigue Might Be Low Iron, Too details the story of my own misdiagnosis and relates how, after five long years of unbelievable physical pain and emotional anguish, I recovered in just a few weeks with the help of iron. Part personal history, and part medical treatise, the book discloses, through patient histories and scientific evidence, how and why the remarkably common but oft-hidden state of iron deficiency is frequently mistaken for other conditions.

It's the Iron is the first book to uncover this major public health issue that affects many millions. I'm very passionate about this project and can't wait to release it! Alas, a book of this type requires a copious amount of writing and research, and it will be some months yet before it's complete. You can keep track of my progress by subscribing to my newsletter (http://eepurl.com/OYNDL) or following my blog (lorilschafer.com), both of which I will be updating with snippets from the book as well as interesting bits of research I've uncovered in the course of my quest. In the meantime, feel free to send me an email at lorilschafer(at)outlook(dot)com – I'd love to hear your story, too!

STORIES FROM MY MEMORY-SHELF: FICTION AND ESSAYS FROM MY PAST

The story of my life told in short fiction and essays. Features author commentary on the real-life events that inspired the stories.

Now available in paperback (both standard and large print sizes) and eBook from retailers worldwide.

"Girl in Pink, Seeing Red"
Never mess with a little girl's best friend – even if she is dressed all in pink.
Micro fiction. Includes author commentary.

"Two Fathers"

"He is clasping my hand and leading me down the street to the local bar; propping me up on a barstool so all his friends can see, can joke with me and about me while I twirl about on the red vinyl, tall and proud to be out with Daddy."
Vignette. Includes commentary on the fathers from my youth.

"Yellow Wagon"
A young girl walks to school alone – is she being stalked?
Flash fiction. Includes an alternate version and my essay "How Many Times Do I Have to Rewrite this %&^# Thing? The 'Yellow Wagon Saga"

"The Second Grade"
"One early autumn afternoon my new friend Amanda taught me some cheerleading moves she'd copied from TV and then convinced me to assist her in putting on a show for the boys of the neighborhood.

After the unremarkable entertainment she approached me, her eyes glistening. 'Did you notice how when I was up there on the picnic table, the boys were all interested and excited and stuff?'

'Sure,' I said. I had, of course, noticed no such thing. I'd been far too busy concentrating on what was, to me, a complicated choreography.

'And when you were up there, did you see how they sat with their heads down, kind of bored?' She smiled broadly when she said it.

'Sure,' I agreed, not wanting to sound as if I had overlooked something so important, and for the first time wondering whether I was coordinated or not.

She began kicking her beautifully browned legs high in the air and it was thirty years before I danced in public again."
Personal essay. Because everything's a first when you're in the second grade.

"Twilight"
"She was strong, she was beautiful, she was graceful. Even if it was only in twilight that it showed."
My very first flash fiction publication. Includes author commentary.

"Past and Present"
" 'It was lucky I forgot my keys,' her mother was saying, rubbing the raised scar between her daughter's thumb and forefinger. 'I came back and found you lying in a pool of blood.' "
Flash fiction. Third place winner of *Avalon Literary Review*'s Summer 2013 Contest. Includes author commentary.

"Haunted"
"Large for my age, prideful of my tomboyhood, and assured in my paranormal incredulity, it was I who braved the deep, I, even, who had relayed the tale of the enigmatic contents of the newspaper room following my first venture there, and inadvertently set the neighborhood to wondering what horrors might be lurking at its bottom."
Essay. In which rationality triumphs over superstition – almost.

"Goat"
" 'What's the matter, Sutton?' Mr. Jenkins inquired. 'Schneider get your goat?'
    There was a momentous silent pause followed by the audible snap of thirty heads whipping around in unison towards the mortified young girl and the shamelessly grinning boy who had yanked on her ponytail until she'd finally shouted at him to quit it."
Flash fiction. Includes commentary on how acquiring an odious nickname changed my adolescent life for the better.

"Fallen Ideal"
"I didn't think I wanted to get married. But now I wonder who will take me to the bathroom when I'm too old to stand."
Micro fiction. Includes author commentary on why married people live longer.

"Deep-Water Girl"
"Go on, deep-water girl! Keep on lookin' for that deep water! You won't never find it!"
Micro fiction. Includes commentary on "deep-water man" and one of my more bizarre travel experiences.

"Rest Stop"

"He approached her, thumbs tucked into the pockets of his own full-length dungarees, evidently immune to the heat.
'Say, that's an expensive trip,' he observed. 'You, uh – you got enough money to get there?' "
Flash fiction. Includes commentary on my first time being propositioned as a body for hire – and how long it took me to realize that that's what had happened.

"Found Money"
"It was something, wasn't it? Finding five dollars. Not a matter of life or death, maybe. Not just yet."
Flash fiction. Includes commentary on one of the most trying times of my life, my homeless period.

"Heads of the Line"
"Each job had its own rhythm. Scrape, scrape, scrape. Thunk; thunk; thunk. It was such a persuasive rhythm that sometimes you even forgot that it was a part of the job. Like that unfortunate header from last season…"
Flash fiction. Includes commentary on my months working in an Alaskan fish-packing plant.

"Fog Line"
"He raised his flashlight and looked her over, as they always did, comparing the image on the out-of-state license to the young woman in the rusty van that pre-dated her by a decade."
Flash fiction. Includes author commentary on being a recurring "victim" of vehicular profiling.

"Jackson, Mississippi"
"An unremarkable middle-aged woman was sunk into the plastic chair outside of the room next to mine, her elbows crushed upon her knees, deeply engaged in smoking a thin, brown cigarette. I nodded politely and so did she and that was when it hit me that she was the first white person I'd seen in hours, perhaps all day."
Essay on momentraily understanding how it must feel to be black in a largely white world.

"Baby and Me"

"Our best friends were having a baby. Inwardly, I groaned."
Flash fiction. In which I fail to comprehend the reproductive instinct that seems to be consuming everyone around me.

"Funeral for Charlie"
"I watched as the water swirled away, taking Charlie on one final miraculous journey to the home of his ancient ancestors, to the ocean the abrupt end of his short life had precluded him from ever going to see."
Flash fiction. Sad, but oh so true.

"Dead in the Water"
"She hung suspended, gazing up at the sky, the sun, the surface, at the cord entangling her foot. It was too late. She would drown; she would die there beneath the water, ten feet away from the people who loved her."
Micro-fiction. Includes commentary on the day that changed the course of my life forever.

"Scars"
An exploration of the map of my body.
Essay. Includes author commentary. "Youth does not have a fair picture of itself... It is only with the perspective of years that we begin to see our lives in patterns, in great sweeping arcs that promise, if we examine them closely, to reveal to us something of ourselves, something of who we were, something of who we have become. Something of who we will become."

Stories from My Memory-Shelf: Fiction and Essays from My Past

Now available in paperback and eBook from retailers worldwide.

ABOUT THE AUTHOR

LORI SCHAFER IS a writer of serious prose, humorous erotica and romance, and everything in between. Her flash fiction, short stories, and essays have appeared in numerous print and online publications, and her memoir *On Hearing of My Mother's Death Six Years After It Happened: A Daughter's Memoir of Mental Illness* won a Gold Medal in the 2015 eLit Book Awards. Her latest project, *It's the Iron: How My Iron Deficiency Was Misdiagnosed as Arthritis, and Why Your Depression, Fibromyalgia, Anxiety, and Chronic Pain and Fatigue Might Be Low Iron, Too,* is scheduled for publication in 2018.

When she isn't writing (which isn't often), Lori enjoys playing ice hockey, attending beer festivals, and spending long afternoons reading at the beach in the sunshine.

To receive special offers from Lori, please visit her website at http://lorilschafer.com, where you may subscribe to her newsletter (http://eepurl.com/OYNDL) or follow her blog. You are also welcome to email her directly at lorilschafer(at)outlook(dot)com with any comments, questions, or suggestions you may have. No requests for advice on your love life, however. She'll give it to you, but you probably won't be thrilled with the results.

Website: http://lorilschafer.com

Twitter: http://twitter.com/LoriLSchafer/

Facebook: http://www.facebook.com/lorilschafer/

Pinterest: http://www.pinterest.com/lorilschafer/

Instagram: https://www.instagram.com/lorilschafer/

Amazon: http://www.amazon.com/Lori-Schafer/e/B00MC1UI16/

GooglePlus: http://plus.google.com/u/0/105878636247618615880/

Linked In: http://www.linkedin.com/pub/lori-schafer/67/30a/b64/

Goodreads:
https://www.goodreads.com/author/show/4392104.Lori_Schafer/

YouTube:
http://www.youtube.com/channel/UCb5RugrJMSHh6_4hkgHmkMA/

lorilschafer.com

"We Are All Miss America"

BULK ORDERS AND PERSONAL APPEARANCES

Booksellers interested in carrying *On Hearing of My Mother's Death Six Years After It Happened* or any of Lori's other books should contact Lori directly via email at lorilschafer@outlook.com.

To inquire about discounted bulk orders of *On Hearing of My Mother's Death* for use in classrooms, book clubs, etc., please email Lori at lorilschafer@outlook.com.

The author is available for speaking engagements and other personal appearances in the San Francisco Bay Area and beyond.

On Hearing of My Mother's Death is also available in LARGE PRINT (18-point font) at online retailers worldwide.

BOOK CLUB QUESTIONS

1. What were your favorite and least favorite parts of the book? Were there sections you felt uncomfortable reading, and if so, why?

2. Have you or a loved one ever been diagnosed with any type of mental illness? How did that make you feel?

3. Mood disorders such as depression and anxiety are far more common than psychotic disorders. What are the biggest differences between the two? Are there similarities, too?

4. What do you think of the choices Lori made in coping with her mother's illness?

5. What else might she have done?

6. How do you think you would have responded in her situation?

7. How would you want your loved ones to respond if you were afflicted with a severe mental illness?

8. A recurring theme in Lori's memoir is the powerlessness she felt because of her youth. What do you think could be done to better ensure the safety of minors whose parents are abusive or unstable?

9. How do you think the experiences of children with parents with mental illness differ from those of children whose parents struggle with substance abuse? How are they the same?

10. How do the experiences of sufferers of willful child abuse or

neglect differ from those of children whose parents cannot control their behavior?

11. Were you surprised that Lori's mother never received the treatment she needed? Was there any way this could have been prevented?

12. How do you think the perception of mental illness differs from the perception of physical illness? Does this perception affect the way the mentally ill are treated? Could it affect their willingness to seek help for their affliction?

13. How would Lori's experience have differed had she had a more extended family?

14. Lori received very little assistance from adults during her mother's illness. Should other adults have interfered more aggressively in her situation? Or can you understand their reluctance to get involved?

15. What did you think of Lori's plan to run away from home? Could she have handled it better?

16. Lori writes in some detail about being homeless and hungry. Have you ever been in a position similar to hers, or thought you might end up that way? Could you imagine what it might be like?

17. If Lori's mother were still alive, would you have liked to see Lori ultimately reunited with her? Why or why not?

18. What did you think of the theme of Lori's "I Am Subject" essay? Are there painful events in your past that feel as though they happened to someone else?

19. Do you think it's better to repress painful memories or to talk about them? Why?

20. Lori's memoir has been called a "survivor's story." What are some other kinds of survivor's stories? Why is it important to tell them?

ENDNOTES

[1] American Psychiatric Association, "What is Schizophrenia?," reviewed by Ranna Parekh, M.D., January 2017, https://www.psychiatry.org/patients-families/schizophrenia/what-is-schizophrenia, accessed 6/26/17.

[2] Torrey, E. Fuller, M.D., *"Surviving Schizophrenia: A Manual for Families, Consumers, and Providers*, Quill: New York, 2001, p. 90.

[3] Ibid.

[4] WebMd, "Schizophrenia: An Overview," reviewed by Joseph Goldberg, MD, January 27, 2015, http://www.webmd.com/schizophrenia/guide/mental-health-schizophrenia#1, accessed 6/26/17.

[5] Folsom, David P., "Schizophrenia in Late Life: Emerging Issues," *Dialogues in Clinical Neuroscience*, 2006 Mar; 8(1): 45–52, https://www.ncbi.nlm.nih.gov/pmc/articles/PMC3181756/, accessed 6/26/17.

[6] Torrey, p. 121.

[7] Ibid., p. 126.

[8] Cockburn, Patrick & Henry, *Henry's Demons*, Scribner: New York, 2011.

[9] WebMd, "Mental Health and Delusional Disorder," May 18, 2016, http://www.webmd.com/schizophrenia/guide/delusional-disorder#1, accessed 6/26/17.

[10] Ibid.

[11] Ibid.

[12] Torrey, p. 93.

[13] Ibid., p. 95-103.

[14] Ibid., p. 94.

[15] Ibid., p. 65.

[16] Ibid., p. 143.

[17] Ibid., p. 364.

[18] Ibid., p. 143-152.

[19] Ibid., p. 108-113.

[20] WebMd, "Schizophrenia: An Overview," http://www.webmd.com/schizophrenia/guide/mental-health-schizophrenia#1, accessed 6/26/17.

[21] Cockburn, p. 95.

[22] Ibid., p. 189.

[23] Torrey, p. 307.

[24] Cockburn, p. 189.

[25] Torrey, p. 307.

[26] American Psychiatric Association, "What are Dissociative Disorders?," reviewed by Philip Wang. M.D., January 2016, https://www.psychiatry.org/patients-families/dissociative-disorders/what-are-dissociative-disorders, accessed 6/27/17.

[27] Ibid.

[28] Torrey, p. 365.

[29] Ibid., p. 80.

[30] Ibid., p. 68.

[31] Ibid., p. 79.

Made in the USA
San Bernardino, CA
12 March 2018